THE BOOK
OF
PLANTERS

FRONTISPIECE: Imaginative use of planters can produce striking decorative effects. (*Courtesy, Flower* ROCHE

THE BOOK
OF
PLANTERS

by
Robert Scharff

M. BARROWS AND COMPANY, INC.
New York   1960

Printed in the United States of America

Published simultaneously in the Dominion of
Canada by George J. McLeod Limited, Toronto
Library of Congress Catalog Card Number: 59–15143

TABLE OF CONTENTS

THE BOOK
OF
PLANTERS

ONE • A New Idea in Gardening

Growing plants in "planters" is an entirely new concept in home gardening that is increasing in popularity by leaps and bounds. To those not familiar with this type of gardening, the first question that logically comes to mind is, "What is a planter?" In the simplest terms, a planter is any container that will hold a plant, and planter gardening therefore ranges from potted palms to indoor gardens. In this book we will be primarily concerned with the type of planter that can be used as an integral part of the decorative scheme of a house, both indoors and out.

One reason for the great popularity of planters today is that contemporary architectural planning, both in the house and outdoors, tends to create innumerable settings and backgrounds appropriate for plant display. For example, inside the home, planters may be successfully used as room dividers, traffic directors, built-in screens and decorative conversation pieces. Any one of these planter units can do much to brighten a room, create a mood or, indeed, change a family's habits. Some friends of mine installed a planter unit between their kitchen and dining room to create a breakfast area, and found that it changed the entire structure of their table conversation. Instead of run-of-the-mill discussions of what had happened at school or work, their talk centered around the progress of the philodendron and wagers on whether the new leaf unfurling on the dieffenbachia would be green, yellow or white. The popularity of this unit led the family to set up arrangements in the other rooms of their house—a large container of green and variegated plants in the den, a planter bin with tropical foliage in the living room, and a small unit with African violets on their daughter's dressing table.

The idea of integrating plants and architecture goes back in our history to the time when California was still part of Mexico and when a patio was just a roofless room with vine-covered walls, decorated with oleanders and orange trees in tubs. Since this early beginning, the West Coast has pioneered the concept of living with plants, and contemporary architecture has spread the trend from California to Maine and Texas. Large glassed-in areas and picture windows, originally styled to bring more of the outdoors indoors, are also responsible for the increasing popularity of interior planters. But possibly more important has been our discovery that plants are structural forms with important design value. The stark horizontal and vertical lines of modern homes need some eye-easing curves added to balance the design, and homeowners are discovering that plants are an easy, pleasant and harmonious way to achieve this softening effect. Actually, the glass wall and the picture window, or the old bay window with floor-to-ceiling glass installed, are natural locations for an indoor planter garden—a floor planting which closely resembles an outdoor garden. The planter area may measure only 2' wide and 5' long, but even within this small area, house plants can give the illusion of a tropical jungle or a northern woods.

An interior planter may be of any size and any shape. In a friend's house there is a planter I have always admired extending across one end of the living room, with the planter edge curving along the bay window inside like the perennial border that blooms outside the glass wall in summer. This planter garden is wide enough to have a brick path winding through it, which makes the garden seem even wider and aids the owner in tending the plants.

A decorative fountain provides the necessary moisture for the plants. In the garden dwarf orange trees bearing bright fruit are placed close to snow-white narcissuses, purple colchicums peep from the soil and a clerodendron vine forms a graceful arch; gloxinias, marantas and pothos provide more color, while two Norfolk Island pines, three furry-trunked Hawaiian tree ferns and clivia add foliage contrast. An indoor planter, of course, need not be as complex as this one.

In the dining room of the same home, the owner has arranged a trellis-and-basket planter with pothos and gloriosa vines, stately calla lilies, camellias, colchicums and a few small, glossy-leaved holly plants to create a charming effect in a simple planter arrangement.

Contrary to popular belief, planters are not limited to homes of contemporary design; a well-designed planter will look as well in an Early American home as a modern one. Another popular misconception about planters is that they must be installed during construction and therefore cannot be used successfully in an already completed house. There are no limits to the ways you can use planters in remodeling work. Not only will they conceal a standing radiator, but very often may be used to cover up a structural defect that cannot be eliminated by remodeling. Do you have a long hallway that seems bleak? Or a corner that does not get much light? Then install wall planters filled with tropical foliage and highlighted by artificial lighting. Remember, many plants will sparkle and thrive in fluorescent light.

Outdoors, the planter has a variety of uses, too. The many illustrations in this book show planters being used for color accent on terraces, porches and patios or along paths and near entrances. With portable planters, you can ring changes in decorative effects as quickly as you can rearrange the furniture in your room. Planters also provide a practical method of maintaining a smooth succession of color in your garden, instead of the usual feast or famine of bloom. A planter garden can be controlled more easily and more directly than a flower bed.

Portable planters are very popular with people living in rented houses and apartments. You can use planters to cover up the bareness of a room or garden without going to the expense of making permanent plantings. With these portable containers, you can enjoy all the benefits and joys of planter gardening and take them with you, should you move.

To some gardeners, planter gardening sounds like a lot of work, but after trying it, they soon discover the reverse is usually the case. When plants are concentrated in an area close at hand, watering, feeding and other maintenance jobs are more easily controlled.

This book is intended to be a simple, down-to-earth guide to the fascinating hobby of planter gardening. After reading it carefully, pick the design best suited to your purpose, construct it, plant it and patiently care for the plants. Your efforts will be richly rewarded by the beauty your planter will bring to a room or outdoor area.

TWO • Portable Planters

Once you have decided that you would like to try your hand at the fascinating hobby of planter gardening, your first task will be to construct a planter. Here you have a choice between two basic types of planters—built-in and portable. This chapter will discuss the portable planter, and the following chapter will consider the built-in variety.

With your foliage and flowering plants boxed, tubbed or

barreled, you can rearrange them just as you would move the furniture in your home. Such portable planters are ideal for people living in rented houses, apartments or summer homes, who want the beauty of plants but do not wish to build permanent planter units. Outdoors, portable planters are very useful as color accents on decks, patios, porches and terraces or along paths and entranceways. And most important they are the simplest method of producing quick color in your landscape. Whenever you notice a place that is blank and colorless, move in a plant in a portable planter and watch the landscape suddenly come to life.

While portable planters are primarily used outdoors, they also play an important part in interior decoration. Mobile units are the answer if your window space is too limited for growing all the house plants you would like or if sunny windows are at a premium in your house. Making your planters portable is a wonderful way to be assured of fresh arrangements of plants from week to week. Also, such planters can be kept outdoors during the summer months and then taken inside for the winter.

Almost any type of container can be used as a portable planter, so long as it meets the following requirements:
1. ample volume
2. good drainage
3. strength (you will want to move the planters several times a year and moist soil is heavy)
4. a wide base (so it will not tip over easily)
5. rust-and-rot resistant (painted metal or chemically treated wood)

This means you can use wooden boxes and tubs; large clay pots, which can be decorative in themselves and big tin cans, which can be painted or decorated with rope, twine or rectangular flue tiles to improve their appearance. The general shape of the plants at maturity should, if possible, determine the shape of the container. Plants with a sphere of foliage on a straight stem should be placed in low planters; squat, bushy plants look best in low, square containers; plants with tapering forms belong in tall units.

POTS

Pots can be as exciting as the plants they hold. A well-designed composition is the goal to strive for: the right plant, the right container and the right location. The possibilities are endless. As you become plant- and planter-conscious, your ideas will multiply rapidly. A quick trip to the five-and-ten and a visit to the florist will provide you with a variety of pots. Materials include clay, plastic, Fiberglas, brass, aluminum, cast iron, terra cotta and glass.

Clay Pots

When the pots are to be set into peat or sphagnum moss, or vermiculite, unglazed red clay is generally recommended. Unglazed pots are available in a wide range of sizes and shapes. The "standard" pot is the one generally used in both stationary and portable planters. "Standard" means that the pot is as wide at the top as it is high; for example, 6″ wide by 6″ high. These are obtainable in sizes beginning at 1″ wide and ranging up to 16″ wide. The larger sizes over 10″ are generally referred to as tubs.

The three-quarter pot is three-quarters as high as it is wide; that is, a 6″ wide pot would be 4½″ high. Pots half as tall as they are wide are known as "pans." These last two types—pans and three-quarter pots—are generally preferred by many people for interior planters because their wide bases make them more stable.

The tar-paper cylinders used so much by nurserymen to save the cost of regular clay flowerpots, are growing in popularity with outdoor planter gardeners. These tar-paper pots are not very handsome, but they can be painted, or easily slipped into decorative boxes or tubs for display purposes. Their greatest advantage is that they are inexpensive (about 10 cents each), and easy to move about.

Ceramic Pots

Ceramic or glazed pots are very versatile. They may be placed in shallow stationary planters where the pots will be seen, or they may be used alone as portable planters. They come in many shapes and sizes and in an infinite variety of textures and colors. Soft, subdued pastel colors like yellow, blue, pink, green, white, etc., are preferable to harsh colors, and a plain-textured finish gives a better effect than a distracting decoration. When judiciously selected, ceramic pots will blend most pleasantly with the plants they hold and with the décor of a room. But some indoor planter gardeners find there is the danger of overwatering plants in glazed pots because there is no drainage hole and the sides are not porous. However, you can enjoy the good looks of a ceramic pot without the drainage problem by fitting a clay pot inside to hold the plants.

WOODEN PLANTER BOXES

Of all portable containers, the wooden box is the most versatile for use in any decorative scheme, either inside or out. Many a homeowner has wished for a convenient way to dress up his garden or living room for a special occasion or to keep an area constantly at the peak of bloom. Rotating planting schedules, pot gardening and even stationary planter units (Chapter 3) provide only a partial solution. But by the simple scheme of using replaceable planter boxes, an ever-blooming garden is assured even for the novice.

With the planter-box system, even the apartment dweller can keep his terrace in perpetual bloom or his rooms filled with beautiful greens. The system hinges on using boxes of similar size and design. When the blooming period of one group of plants is over, those boxes are removed and other boxes of the same size containing plants just coming into bloom are brought in from the nursery or the private hothouse as replacements. Planter boxes may be used singly, in groups, in rows or in masses to create a variety of arrangements or even furnish a whole garden. If desired, the boxes may be painted or stained to match the color of the house or the room.

Planter boxes can be used at the edge of a terrace or patio, against an exterior wall or a fence, and around a tree well or a pool. When placed along garden paths or walks, they can direct the flow of traffic—for example, pointing out one way to the front door, another to a side entrance.

Construction of Wooden Planter Boxes

These planters can be bought ready-made or can be built by the gardener or ordered from the local woodworking shop. Most department stores and garden-supply outlets carry a variety of wooden planter boxes. Whether you build your own boxes or buy them ready-made, make sure they are of a durable wood such as redwood, cedar, cypress or exterior-type fir plywood. Other kinds of wood are usable for portable planter boxes, but they must be thoroughly treated with a nonpoisonous wood preservative to prevent rapid deterioration and decay.

There are many designs for portable planter boxes and several methods of construction may be used. In general, however, standard modular boxes are quickest and most easily made. In addition they are rugged and practical and can be stacked when empty. Their proportions are multiples of eight, that is 8″ by 8″, 8″ by 16″, 8″ by 24″, 8″ by 32″, 16″ by 16″ and so on (Fig. 1). One of these boxes used singly is effective in its own right. Used in multiples of one size or in mixed sizes, they may be placed in a variety of geometric patterns as shown in Plate 1. To achieve the full effect of matched planter arrangements, you will need to use at least four of each size. The height of the boxes may vary from 4″ to 24″ but it is a good idea to make the majority of them all the same size.

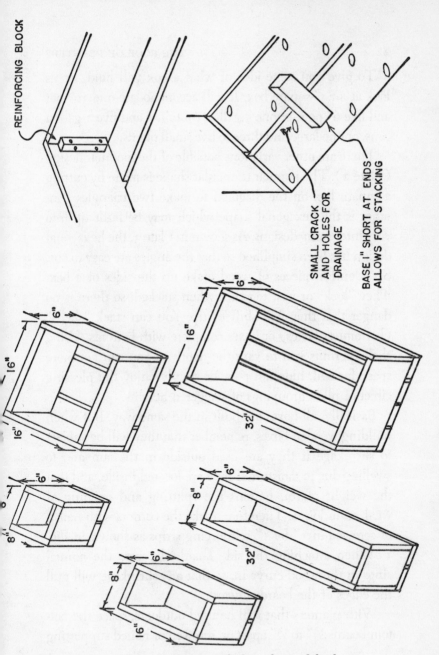

REINFORCING BLOCK

SMALL CRACK AND HOLES FOR DRAINAGE

BASE 1" SHORT AT ENDS ALLOWS FOR STACKING

Fig. 1: Construction details for standard wooden modular boxes.

To give you some idea of what a box will hold, let us look at a 24"-square box. It will accommodate one 10" pot and five 6" pots, or one 5-gallon container and five 1-gallon cans, or one large and three to five small plants.

There are other variations possible of the modular design (Plate 2). The popular triangular shape is made by cutting a square box on the diagonal to make two triangles. Another is the hexagonal shape which may be built up into very interesting designs. As shown in Plate 3, the hexagonal design has been simplified so that the angles are easy to cut. Six identical pieces of wood make up the sides of a box. They "lock" or nest together when stacked, so there is no danger that they will shift or tip. You can stack "shells" (bottomless boxes) or boxes complete with bottoms. Using shells permits you to vary the depth so you can get more space for soil, hide tall pots, or simply enjoy the pleasing effect of plant groupings of staggered heights.

Basically, all boxes are built in the same way. But when building wooden boxes, remember that they will be subject to shrinkage if they are used outside in the sun and to swelling due to moisture if they are located inside, and that the weight of soil hastens the splitting and opening of weak seam joints. Therefore, make the corners with nailed or screwed-in 1" by 1" reinforcing strips as shown in Fig. 1. When attaching the side boards, be sure the annual rings in the wood curve in, so that any shrinkage will pull the edges of the boards inward.

With planters that will be used outdoors, space the bottom boards ¼" to ½" apart on screwed or nailed supporting cleats. The cleats will permit air circulation under the box, retard rot and allow better drainage. The holes for drainage should be ½″ to ¾″ in diameter. Elevating the planter by putting cleats on the bottom of the box is also effective from the standpoint of appearance, and the cleats will make the boxes easier to lift. If necessary, waterproof glues may be used for assembling the box. If nails or other hardware are used, they should be of a noncorrosive metal such as aluminum, copper, bronze, brass or galvanized steel. Do not use ordinary steel nails or screws.

When making planter boxes for interior use, leave no space between the bottom boards and omit the drainage holes. Also be sure to use a liner for your interior planter box. Details on liners can be found in Chapter 3.

The choice of lumber for the planter box will depend on the appearance desired. Most popular in use today is rough, unplaned lumber. This can be left its natural color or stained to any desired color with pigmented stains. Many of these stains also have wood-preserving qualities. For painted and more finished effects which require a smooth exterior surface, the lumber should be planed at the mill or lumberyard before the box is constructed. If you use one of the naturally decay resistant woods previously mentioned, no wood preservatives are necessary.

The three plywood planter boxes shown in Plate 5 are also easy to build. The three designs may be combined, or you may arrange similar boxes in a pattern that either complements or contrasts with your setting. (Construction details for these boxes are given in Fig. 2 and Fig. 3.) To

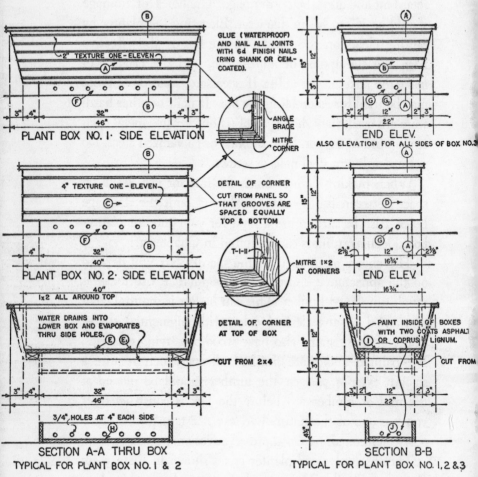

GLUE (WATERPROOF) AND NAIL ALL JOINTS WITH 6d FINISH NAILS (RING SHANK OR CEM.-COATED).

2" TEXTURE ONE-ELEVEN

PLANT BOX NO. 1· SIDE ELEVATION

32"
46"
3" 4"
4" 3"

END ELEV.
ALSO ELEVATION FOR ALL SIDES OF BOX NO.3

12"
15"
3"
3" 2"   2" 3"
22"

ANGLE BRACE
MITRE CORNER

DETAIL OF CORNER
CUT FROM PANEL SO THAT GROOVES ARE SPACED EQUALLY TOP & BOTTOM

4" TEXTURE ONE-ELEVEN

PLANT BOX NO. 2· SIDE ELEVATION

4"
32"
40"
4"

T-1-11

MITRE 1×2 AT CORNERS

DETAIL OF CORNER AT TOP OF BOX

CUT FROM 2×4

END ELEV.
2⅜"   12"   2⅜"
16¾"

15"
12"
3"

40"
1×2 ALL AROUND TOP

WATER DRAINS INTO LOWER BOX AND EVAPORATES THRU SIDE HOLES.

3" 4"
32"
46"
4" 3"

3/4" HOLES AT 4" EACH SIDE

SECTION A-A THRU BOX
TYPICAL FOR PLANT BOX NO. 1 & 2

16¾"

PAINT INSIDE OF BOXES WITH TWO COATS ASPHALT OR COPRUS LIGNUM.

CUT FROM

15"
12"
3"
4½"

3" 2"   12"   2" 3"
22"

SECTION B-B
TYPICAL FOR PLANT BOX NO. 1, 2 & 3

Fig. 2: Construction details for the three modular planters pictured in Plate 5.

PLATE 1: Modular planter boxes are easy to move and can be arranged in a variety of geometric designs. (*Courtesy, California Redwood Association.*)

PLATE 2: These popular triangular-shaped boxes can be made by cutting a square box on the diagonal. (*Courtesy, California Redwood Association; Designer, Kathryn Stedman.*)

PLATE 3: Hexagonal planter boxes are easy to cut because of their simplified design. (*Courtesy, California Redwood Association.*)

PLATE 4: Hexagonal planter boxes stacked at different heights create an interesting design. (*Courtesy, California Redwood Association.*)

PHIL PALMER

PLATE 5: The custom-built look of these three plywood planter boxes does not involve fancy carpentry.

PLATE 6: A truly portable planter unit that can be wheeled around the garden. (*Courtesy, H. A. Bruno and Associates.*)

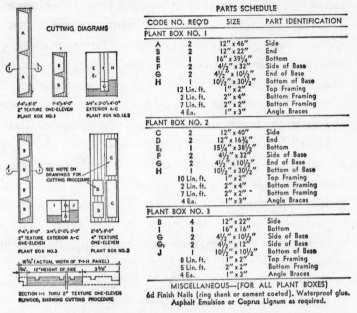

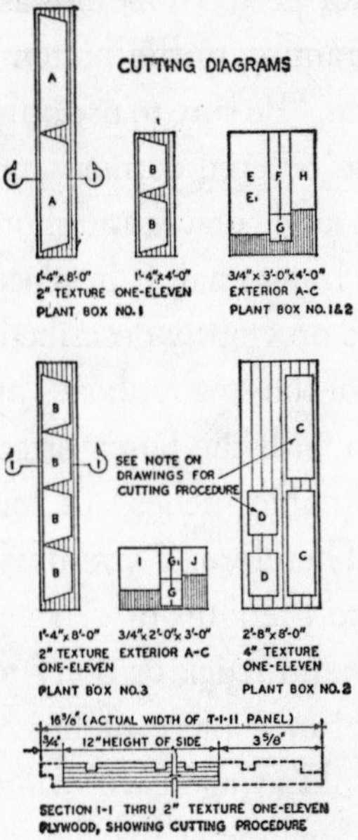
CUTTING DIAGRAMS
A
A
B
B
E
E₁
F
H
G
1'-4" x 8'-0"
2" TEXTURE ONE-ELEVEN
1'-4" x 4'-0"
PLANT BOX NO. 1
3/4" x 3'-0" x 4'-0"
EXTERIOR A-C
PLANT BOX NO. 1 & 2
B
B
B
B
SEE NOTE ON DRAWINGS FOR CUTTING PROCEDURE
I
G₁
J
G
C
D
D
C
1'-4" x 8'-0"
2" TEXTURE ONE-ELEVEN
PLANT BOX NO. 3
3/4" x 2'-0" x 3'-0"
EXTERIOR A-C
2'-8" x 8'-0"
4" TEXTURE ONE-ELEVEN
PLANT BOX NO. 2
16 5/8" (ACTUAL WIDTH OF T-1-11 PANEL)
3/4"
12" HEIGHT OF SIDE
3 5/8"
SECTION 1-1 THRU 2" TEXTURE ONE-ELEVEN PLYWOOD, SHOWING CUTTING PROCEDURE

PARTS SCHEDULE

CODE NO.	REQ'D	SIZE	PART IDENTIFICATION
PLANT BOX NO. 1			
A	2	12" x 46"	Side
B	2	12" x 22"	End
E	1	16" x 39¼"	Bottom
F	2	4½" x 32"	Side of Base
G	2	4½" x 10½"	End of Base
H	1	10½" x 30½"	Bottom of Base
	12 Lin. ft.	1" x 2"	Top Framing
	2 Lin. ft.	2" x 4"	Bottom Framing
	7 Lin. ft.	2" x 2"	Bottom Framing
	4 Ea.	1" x 3"	Angle Braces
PLANT BOX NO. 2			
C	2	12" x 40"	Side
D	2	12" x 16¾"	End
E_1	1	15¼" x 38½"	Bottom
F	2	4½" x 32"	Side of Base
G	2	4½" x 10½"	End of Base
H	1	10½" x 30½"	Bottom of Base
	10 Lin. ft.	1" x 2"	Top Framing
	2 Lin. ft.	2" x 4"	Bottom Framing
	7 Lin. ft.	2" x 2"	Bottom Framing
	4 Ea.	1" x 3"	Angle Braces
PLANT BOX NO. 3			
B	4	12" x 22"	Side
I	1	16" x 16"	Bottom
G	2	4½" x 10½"	Side of Base
G_1	2	4½" x 12"	Side of Base
J	1	10½" x 10½"	Bottom of Base
	8 Lin. ft.	1" x 2"	Top Framing
	5 Lin. ft.	2" x 2"	Bottom Framing
	4 Ea.	1" x 3"	Angle Braces

MISCELLANEOUS—(FOR ALL PLANT BOXES)
6d Finish Nails (ring shank or cement coated). Waterproof glue. Asphalt Emulsion or Coprus Lignum as required.

Fig. 3: Parts schedule and cutting diagrams to supplement construction details given in Fig. 2.

begin constructing the boxes, cut the bottom to size for the box you want to build. The dimensions may be varied to suit your needs. Be sure to use only exterior-type plywood. (Exterior texture one-eleven plywood was used for the planters shown in the illustration.) Next drill drainage holes in the bottom. Then cut the plywood sides and ends to size and make miter joints at the corners. Now, measure and cut the 2″ by 2″ and 2″ by 4″ bottom framing. If you are building Plant Box No. 1 or No. 3, you will need to bevel the sides and cut the bottom framing and bottom panel to conform to the sloping sides. To prevent leaks check the

pieces and make sure they fit together perfectly before assembling. Then glue and nail the framing to the bottom,
and screw or nail the sides to the frame. (Be sure to use only
waterproof adhesive.) Next glue the mitered corners and
clamp the inside together tightly with angle braces and short
screws. Then miter the 1" by 2" top frame, nail it in place
and finish the box in one of the ways previously described.

Usually one person can move one of the smaller boxes by
himself, but he may need some help with the larger sizes.
Remember that a cubic foot (1728 cubic inches) of soil
weighs approximately 100 pounds. Therefore, if you must
move larger boxes frequently, use short lengths of 1" steel
pipe as rollers or a light industrial hand truck or dolly to
make the task easier. A snow shovel or a piece of heavy
burlap can be used as a skid and a child's wagon will come
in handy for long-distance hauling. Sometimes wooden or
rope handles can be designed as an integral part of the box.
For a truly portable planter box, you can construct one on
wheels as illustrated in Plate 6. Sometimes the wheels may
be difficult to buy, but large casters are available in most
hardware stores. Swivel casters (at least 2" in diameter)
may even be preferred because they make it possible to
push the planter in any direction. Swivel casters may be attached to the four corners of the planter bottom, or a pair
of rigid casters may be fastened to one side and a pair of
cleats to the other. With the latter method, the planter is
moved by lifting the side or end with the cleats and rolling
the planter on the casters like a wheelbarrow.

The trellis portion of the roller planter shown in Fig. 4

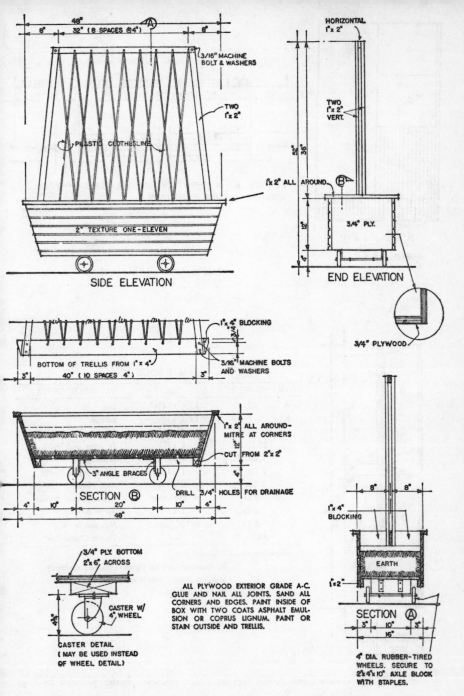

Fig. 4: Construction details for the trellis portable planter pictured in Plate 6.

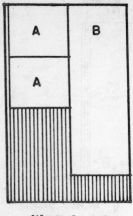

¾" x 2'-6" x 4'-0"

EXTERIOR A-C

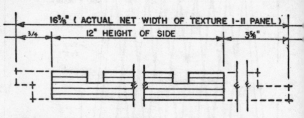

16⅜" (ACTUAL NET WIDTH OF TEXTURE 1-11 PANEL)

¾ 12" HEIGHT OF SIDE 3⅝"

SECTION A – A THRU TEXTURE ONE-ELEVEN PANEL SHOWING CUTTING PROCEDURE.

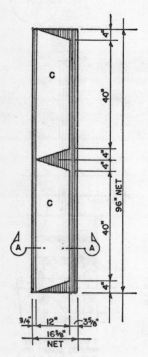

¾ 12" 3⅝"
16⅜"
NET

PARTS SCHEDULE

CODE	NO. REQ'D	SIZE	PART IDENTIFICATION
A	2	12½"x14¾"	End
B	1	14¾"x40½"	Bottom
C	2	12"x48"	Sides
	35 Lin. Ft.	1"x2"	Framing and Trellis
	3 Lin. Ft.	2"x2"	Framing
	7 Lin. Ft.	1"x4"	Blocking and Trellis
	2 Lin. Ft.	2"x4"	Axle Block
	2 Ea.	4" Diameter	Rubber-Tired Wheels
	4 Ea.	1"x3"	Angle Braces
	6 Ea.	3/16" Round	Machine Bolts
	54 Lin. Ft.	—	Plastic Clothesline

Miscellaneous—2 Steel Axles

8d Common and 6d Finish Nails (Galvanized)

Staples, Screws and Washers as required

Waterproof Glue

Fig. 4: Construction details for the trellis portable planter pictured in Plate 6.

is optional. In fact you will notice that it is only bolted together, making it easy to take apart. It would be wise to make the entire planter, including the trellis, which can be stored away if you decide not to use it. Plastic clothesline is called for in the plan because it is very durable and can withstand the rigors of the outdoor exposure. Another reason for using plastic clothesline is that it will not sag when wet, while ordinary clothesline may sag after a very short time.

Other designs for planter boxes may be obtained free of charge by writing to the Service Library, California Redwood Association, 576 Sacramento Street, San Francisco 11, California. Ask for data sheets 3C7-1, "Planter Boxes."

Planting Wooden Planter Boxes

Plants in exterior boxes may be planted in open soil or in pots or containers. Plants for interior boxes should always be planted in pots and set in peat moss or sphagnum moss. The actual planting technique and care for exterior planters is described in Chapter 7 and for interior planters in Chapters 5 and 6. Be sure to bridge the drainage holes in the bottom of an exterior box to prevent the soil from washing out when the plants are watered by placing curved pieces of broken flowerpots or crockery over the holes. Or nail ¼" wire mesh over them. If you do not plan to use moss as a filler around the pots, you will need to place a clump of excelsior or moss over the broken crockery or screen before filling the box with soil. Keep the soil at least 1" below the top of the planter box. Remember, because of the restricted root system, plants in boxes must be watered more often than those growing in ordinary flower beds.

If you plan to rotate the flowering plant units to maintain constant bloom, you will need storage space in some protected location, where the plants can grow until they are ready to be put on view. To care for the plants more easily during this waiting period and to keep them out of the reach of ground pests, place the planter boxes off the ground on benches or on improvised platforms made by laying planks on boxes or sawhorses.

TUBS AND BARRELS

While some true-blue planter gardeners do not consider tubs and barrels proper containers, they do fit the definition we gave to planters in Chapter 1. And these inexpensive containers, when properly treated, make good-looking and durable planters. Small barrels and nail kegs are ideal ready-made containers, both when used full size or cut in half to form two pail-shaped planters. They can also be cut in half lengthwise to make long, shallow planters and fitted with short pipes or wrought-iron legs.

To be used as planters, tubs, barrels and similar containers must be able to withstand sunshine and intermittent watering. They should also be treated to resist rotting and rusting. Drainage holes should be cut out in the bottom of the container to facilitate drainage, and the bottom of the container should be raised off the ground slightly by means of cleats, blocks or legs. The final requirement is that the tub or barrel must be deep enough to hold sufficient soil to allow proper root growth. (Tub and barrel capacity is generally given in liquid measure. To convert gallons to dry measure, multiply by 0.1337. This will give you the number of cubic feet of soil the container will hold, i.e., a 5-gallon container will hold 0.6685 cubic feet of soil.) It is especially important to consider the size of your container when planting small shrubs. For instance, azaleas, bouvardias, gardenias and lantanas usually need a container 12" to 18" deep, while camellias, boxwoods, laurels, kumquats, rhododendrons, and viburnums will require depths of 18" to 24".

Barrels are among the most popular containers in use as planters today. You can find out where to buy one by checking the classified section of your telephone directory under "Barrels and Drums." The cost of new barrels may vary from $2 for the 5-gallon size to $10 for the 55-gallon size. Old or reconditioned barrels, however, may be bought for considerably less. For example, a used butter tub which holds about 60 pounds of topsoil is an ideal container for growing shrubs or small trees for several years. As a matter of fact, I have used more than a hundred butter tubs and 50-pound lard tins as portable planters and have grown all manner of flowering shrubs, fruit trees and vines in them.

To convert a barrel into a planter, first remove the top. This can be done by hammering gently all around the top ring of the barrel, lifting out the top and replacing the ring. This will give you a planter that is the full height of the barrel. However, if you want a shorter planter, saw through the barrel after first marking around its belly with a chalk line at the desired height. Then place a cleat on the inside of the bottom of the barrel so that the weight of soil will not rest on the edges of the staves, the weakest part of the barrel. It is necessary to bore holes in the bottom for drainage as with any other container. Bore one ¾" hole for each square foot of bottom surface. It is a good idea to put tacks under each hoop on the barrel to hold them in position.

To complete the barrel planter, coat the inside with an asphalt emulsion or some other wood preservative and paint or stain the outside. Whenever possible, get barrels with galvanized hoops. Black iron hoops must be painted or they will rust very quickly.

To make tubs and barrels portable, you may put casters on the base or make plant "walkers." (Walkers are platforms with wheels as shown in Plate 7.) The latter arrangement is best for interior use because it has a built-in drainage dish under the platform.

If you want to use metal containers, cut them to the desired size and punch several drainage holes in the bottom. Fasten a couple of 2" by 2" wood blocks to the bottom to allow air circulation underneath the container. You can dress up a metal container by making a fluted edge around the top with a pair of pliers. Then paint the container to harmonize with your setting.

Another way to use a metal container is make a wooden "topcoat" for it. To do this, cut some narrow pieces of wood the height of the container plus the wooden block fastened to its bottom. Then wire the wood pieces together with thin wire at the top and bottom. Stapling is an easy way to attach the wire to the pieces of wood. Twist the ends of the wire together on the inside to hold the "topcoat" in place and slip it over the container.

When planting a tub, barrel or metal container, follow the same procedure as previously described for wooden boxes. To keep the soil from plugging the drainage openings, put broken pottery, flat stones or gravel in the bottom. Setting a shrub or tree into such a container is a fairly simple task when the roots are enclosed in a ball of soil covered with burlap. First, soak the root ball in a bucket of water, then gently lower the burlaped ball into the container, setting it on a cushion of soil (use the average mixture given in Chapter 8) over a layer of gravel or stones. The top of the root ball should be approximately 2" below the top of the container. If the plant sits too high, remove a little soil; if it sits too low, remove the plant and fill in with additional soil. Before covering the root ball, cut the twine that holds the burlap around the trunk. Leave the burlap in place since it will rot away quickly. Cover the top with additional soil and soak thoroughly.

FLUE TILE AND BLOCK PLANTERS

Flue or gutter drain tiles of durable, weatherproof clay, in soft colors, make excellent portable planters for both interior and exterior decorative use. These tiles come in square and round shapes with 8" to 24" openings and in lengths of 12" and 24". The tiles can be cut to any desired size with a hammer and cold chisel.

Once cut to size, tile planters can either be set on a wood

base or fitted with wooden bottoms. The top edges can be trimmed with wood or metal or left as they are. The plants are put in pots which are set in the containers and the remaining space is filled with peat moss or sphagnum moss.

Cinder or concrete blocks can be salvaged from construction projects and used as planters, of sorts. A patio block planter is an inexpensive decorative addition to an outdoor living area. Simply border your patio area with cinder or concrete blocks set end-to-end, then fill the openings with the average soil mixture. Plant the blocks with your favorite flowering plants or foliage. Finish by painting the blocks with masonry paint to blend with your decorative scheme.

HANGING PLANTERS

Of the many advantages of using hanging planters, the two most important are that they put flowers and foliage at eye level and offer more planting space in a limited area. And hanging masses of greens and flowers will add a luxuriant look to any wall surface. The staghorn fern (*Platycerium*) shown in Plate 8 has been used successfully in hanging containers both indoors and out. The fern is placed in sphagnum moss in a wire container, or on a moisture-retaining slab of wood. It has been known to withstand extremely low temperatures down to 27 degrees F., but, of course, the fern is a tropical plant that really needs warm temperatures for good growth.

In point of fact, this method of planter culture is a form of hydroponics: the growing of plants in chemical nutrient solutions. But, instead of immersing the root systems in water, sphagnum moss is used. The moss retains water, which absorbs and stores the nutrients necessary for plant growth. The moss also acts as a buffer that prevents an over-concentration of salts due to over-fertilizing.

The construction of containters suitable for soilless plant culture is simple. They may be almost any size and shape. The skeleton may be constructed of metal or durable wood (cypress, cedar or redwood). If other types of wood are used, treat them with a rot-resistant, nonpoisonous preservative. If metal is used, treat it to prevent rust and corrosion from fertilizing materials. The frame may be constructed so that all sides are open, making it possible to plant all areas and use the container as a centerpiece. A container with a solid back can be hung from or placed against a wall. Wire grill, metal rods or wood bars are used as backing to support the sphagnum moss in the container. The backing material is set around the open sides and fastened to the frame. If wire grill is used, heavy staples will serve to fasten it to the frame. The top of the container should be left open, as with an ordinary soil planter. If the container is used indoors, a small tray should be attached to the bottom to catch excess water.

Naturally, other materials can be used in place of sphagnum moss. You can use fine peat moss in the center and a coarse, fibrous peat moss for the outer walls. Osmunda fiber or orchid peat is another possibility. All materials should be moistened before they are planted.

When planting, a layer of sphagnum moss (or other material) is placed at the bottom of the container, about 1″

deep. The plant is then inserted in the moss through the openings on the vertical wall. It is advisable to place each plant deeply and at a slight upward slant. Successive layers of plant material and sphagnum moss are built up until the top of the container is reached. Where the container is open on more than one side, all sides should be planted at the same time. The sphagnum moss should be packed firmly at the beginning to avoid a settling reaction later. Some planter gardeners first line the container with sphagnum moss, then fill it with soil. They claim this holds moisture better, especially in wood-slat containers.

The number of plants needed will depend upon the varieties used. You may place the plants close together, since they will not spread like plants in regular horizontal beds. Although more plants are required for moss culture than for soil culture, the cost is offset by the size of the plants used. Rooted cuttings or young plants in 2½″ pots are recommended for soilless containers. Vigorous seedlings also can be used. They are easy to plant and adapt faster than larger plants.

Be sure that your hanging planter is suspended from a substantial hook that will hold the weight of the container and will not pull out of the wall. Use screw eyes, eyebolts or lag-thread clothesline hooks.

After it is planted, the container should be watered thoroughly and placed in a sheltered location for about a week. Spray the foliage occasionally. Generally, one watering is sufficient before the container is put in its permanent location. The planter gardener will find watering is a simple chore. If the moss feels damp, no watering is necessary. However, in hot sun or exposed, windy locations care should be taken to prevent the sphagnum moss from drying out. This can be partly overcome by putting a clay-pot saucer in the bottom of the container between the moss lining and the soil. (Hanging clay pots dry out less rapidly than wire or wood-slat baskets. If you use new clay pots, be sure to soak them in water thoroughly before planting.) Plants will respond to an occasional syringing with a fine spray.

Often the watering and feeding chores can be done at the same time. If the plants need to be watered prior to fertilizing, do a thorough job and really saturate the moss. Then wait a day or two and fertilize. Fertilizing should be started as soon as the containers are placed in their permanent locations. A complete water-soluble fertilizer, including trace elements, should be used every seven to ten days. At the start you can use a solution half the strength recommended by the manufacturer for house plants, then increase or decrease the amount as necessary. The moss should be damp to facilitate penetration of the nutrient solution, which may mean watering the container the day before fertilizing. Whenever possible fertilize on a cloudy day or late in the afternoon to prevent foliage from burning. Use a sprinkling can with a fine rose to help apply the solution evenly. Hanging baskets should be laid on the ground and left there so that the nutrient solution will penetrate. A light spray after fertilizing is beneficial and will remove fertilizer residue from the foliage.

Many types of plants have been grown in sphagnum-moss planters—ageratums, shrimp plants, bush morning-glories, pansies, fuchsias, ferns, balcony petunias, begonias, lantanas, dwarf marigolds, coleuses, camellias, azaleas, lobelias, geraniums, and other plants that prefer a moist and slightly acid soil. Trailing plants, considered nuisances in the neat border or bed garden, are also ideal for planting in hanging planters. In addition, zebrinas, *Asparagus sprengeri,* alternantheras, strawberries, lemon balm, chives, watercress and mints have all done well. Many of the small, compact annuals can also be used. In fact, it would be a challenge for the gardener to see if he could grow other plant materials in this new form of hydroponic plant culture.

MINIATURE PLANTERS

Miniature gardens can take shape in a wide variety of containers, anything in fact from a large planter box to a teacup. These small-scale landscapes can be used in a variety of ways; for example, to create special effects within the framework of a larger garden, to add color to a patio, or to decorate a coffee table.

If you look around the house, you will probably turn up several suitable containers to use for miniature planters. Or, if you like, you can build a simple box similar to the one shown in Plate 9. This container was constructed of 1″ redwood stock lumber, in the same manner as shown in Fig. 1. The drainage problem is neatly solved by spacing the bottom boards about ⅛″ apart. A ½″ layer of gravel will keep the soil from washing out. Calk or tar all seams except those used for drainage. For indoor arrangements you will need to use a liner.

To make the drainage still better in this type of planter, put a thin layer of charcoal over the gravel to prevent souring, and then a layer of peat moss or vermiculite to absorb water. (Even with these extra materials, indiscriminate day-to-day watering will cause sogginess, because the containers, especially the small dish or plastic type, cannot hold the excess water that will accumulate after the peat moss or vermiculite has been saturated.) After you have installed the peat moss or vermiculite, fill the unit with the average soil mixture up to about ½" below the rim of the container.

The surface of the soil in a miniature arrangement need not be flat. A more attractive planting arrangement can be made if the soil is packed into a miniature mountain at one end of the container. Or, if the planter box is large enough, you can construct a small valley with rolling hills. The terrain can also be greatly enhanced by using pieces of rock in the design. These should be placed so that the lines of the strata run parallel to one another, as they would in a natural rock outcrop. The stones will look best if they are carefully chosen to resemble massive rock formations. Fragments of rock can also be used to build small canyons, although the available space will put a limit on the amount of rock you can use.

When planting the miniature landscape, trees are a major consideration. Dwarf-growing varieties have been found to be most suitable. Do not try to plant normally tall trees with the intention of stunting their growth by the widely known bonsai methods. Bonsai, and its use in Japanese miniature gardens, stems from an entirely different tradition and the Japanese and American styles can rarely be combined with success. Bonsai materials can be used in the planters shown in Fig. 6.

The dwarf trees most suitable for the American type of planter garden we are discussing are those that grow slowly and maintain low-growing habits. Of these, the dwarf Irish juniper (*Juniperus hibernica compressa*) is certainly one of the best. This juniper forms an elongated cone and in fifteen years attains a height of 15″. Two other excellent choices are *Chamaecyparis pisifera nana compacta*, with its blue-green foliage and fan-shaped branches; and the hinoki cypress (*Chamaecyparis obtusa ericoides*), one of the best of the bushy types, which produces a rounded mound of branches and foliage. Many other low-growing trees might be used, but most of them sooner or later require annual pruning to control their size. In addition there are, however, a number of small, flowering alpine shrubs that have a treelike appearance. An excellent specimen in this category is the red-flowered succulent plant, *Crassula sarcocaulis*, with its tiny gnarled and twisted branches.

In selecting other plants to complete your garden, try to introduce as much variety as possible in form, color, type of foliage and time of flowering. Young plants, which have been started in small pots, can be transferred to the planter garden at any time of the year, but the best seasons are

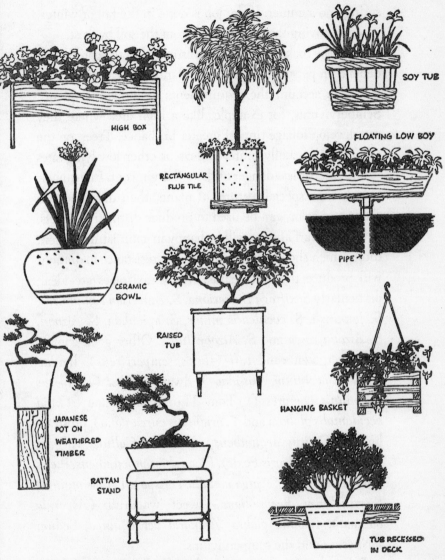

Fig. 6: A selection of typical portable planters. (Courtesy, California Spray-Chemical Corporation.)

spring and summer. If the job is done in the fall or winter, you risk having the plants lifted from the soil by frost.

How the rocks and plants are arranged in the garden will depend on personal taste. But in planning the design, try to take into account the requirements of individual plants. Sempervivums, for example, like a high area where they can develop foliage tints of greater brilliance. Trees, on the other hand, usually prefer valleys or other low-lying sites where there is less danger of the soil drying out. Remember, too, that the special features of plants, their differences in shape and color, can be used to produce distinctive effects.

Many dwarf alpines will be happy in a miniature garden; those which show a certain amount of resistance to drought will produce the best results. Many saxifrages are ideal, particularly *Saxifraga Burseriana*, *S. Burseriana sulphurea*, *S. Jenkinsii*, *S. cochlearis minor*, *S. apiculata*, *S. Aizoon*, *S. Aizoon rosea* and *S. Aizoon lutea*. Other good choices are: evergreen candytuft (*Iberis sempervirens*), lignon-berry (*Vaccinium vitis-idaea*), dwarf juniper (*Juniperus communis compressa*), Tom Thumb arborvitae (*Thuja occidentalis globosa* and *T. orientalis aurea-nana*), prostrate broom (*Cytisus decumbens*), heather (*Calluna vulgaris nana* and *C. vulgaris Foxii*), *Picea abies procumbens*, *Pieris nana*, bugleweed (*Ajuga metallica crispa*), *Erinus alpinus*, *Sisyrinchium Bermudiana*, sweet woodruff (*Asperula odorata*), *Raoulia glabra*, *Arenaria verna aurea*, *Sedum farinosum* and the sempervivums.

Before leaving the subject of small planters, it would be

worthwhile to consider the possibilities of a tray garden. The tray itself is an interior decorator's dream because it can be made to fit a shelf of any size, shape or color. The only parts of the planter tray you will have to construct are the side walls, which are made by nailing 4 strips of wood together. Furring strips 1" by 2" are suitable and may be used to build a frame of any desired size or shape. Place the frame on a shelf where the light will be adequate for plants, either by a window or where there is fluorescent light about 6" above the foliage. Next take a sheet of heavy plastic cloth in a color to suit the room's décor, and lay it on top of the frame so that the edges of the cloth cover the furring strips entirely. This gives you the waterproof floor and side walls for the plant tray. Then fill the tray to the top of the side walls with coarse insulating-grade vermiculite and dampen it completely with the fertilizing water. The plant pots may then be placed on the vermiculite.

OTHER PLANTER IDEAS

The ingenious gardener will find many other containers he can convert into good planters. For example, a large stoneware pickle crock will make an excellent planter, but you must be very careful about drilling the drainage holes in the bottom. An old-fashioned copper wash boiler can be turned into a real conversation piece after it has been polished and filled with a good selection of tropical plants. As other possibilities for unusual containers you might consider using a quaint wooden wheelbarrow, a hollowed-out log, a pot-belly stove, or some small object such as a napkin holder or spoon rack (see Plate 10). You can, of course, build your own novelty piece that will serve as a planter.

Water Trough Planter

The water trough planter (Fig. 7) was made entirely

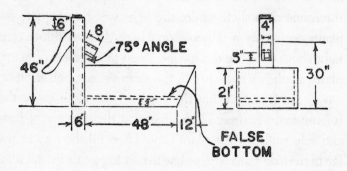

Fig. 7: Construction details for water trough planter.

of ¾" wood except for the pump handle which was cut from 2"-by-6" lumber. The dimensions given in the diagram may be altered. Basically, the planter consists of a long, low box, open at the top, which is built in the shape of an old water trough with a dummy wooden water pump at one end. The pump is made by nailing four pieces of ¾" lumber together to form a column 6" square and 46" high. Before putting the column together, however, cut out the pump handle with a jigsaw or handsaw. Fasten the handle to the back plate of the column by driving large woodscrews through from the inside. The handle should be centered on the back plate about 6" from the top. Also, the water spout should be attached to the front plate of the column before the column is assembled. The spout is made of wood and measures 5" square and 8" long. It should be attached to the front plate at an angle of about 75 degrees and at a point approximately 30" from the ground (see diagram in Fig. 7). Top the finished column with a 4½"-square piece of wood (2" thick) inserted into the hollow of the column about ½" from the top. If you like, you can install a false bottom in the trough 3" from the ground, to make it shallower and reduce the amount of soil needed for planting. Be sure to give all the wood surfaces that will rest on the ground several applications of asphalt.

Wheelbarrow Planter

Because it is easy to move around, the wheelbarrow planter (Fig. 8) can be used to introduce variety and make changes in garden arrangements. Use 2"-by-6" lumber for the main frame arms, which should be about 4' in over-all length. Bring the arms together in a V-shape at one end and mount the wheel at the apex of the V. You will need a slab of wood large enough to cut out a wheel 1' in diameter. This can be made by butt-joining two 14" lengths of 2"-by-6" lumber; use waterproof glue, reinforced with corrugated nails on both sides, to join the pieces. The axle shaft itself can be either ½" or ¾" in diameter. You will need to drill two snug-fitting holes for the axle in the arm brackets and a larger, loose-fitting hole in the wheel.

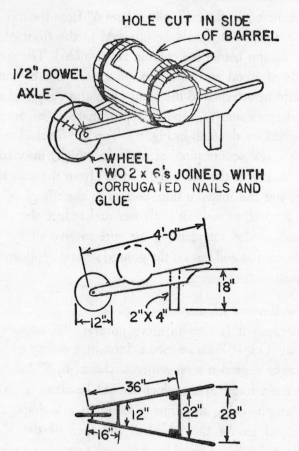

HOLE CUT IN SIDE
OF BARREL

1/2" DOWEL
AXLE

WHEEL
TWO 2 x 6's JOINED WITH
CORRUGATED NAILS AND
GLUE

4'-0"

18"

12"   2"X 4"

36"

12"   22"   28"

16"

Fig. 8: Construction details for wheelbarrow planter.

Since the holes in the main frame, because of its V-shape, will have to be drilled at a slight angle it is best to drill these holes after the frame has been assembled. The completed frame will consist of the two main arms held in their V position by two spreader arms made of 2"-by-4" lumber, one 12" long and the other 22" long. The shorter arm should cross the V at a point 16" from the wheel end, and the other arm should be located about 36" from the wheel end. Slight forward or backward adjustments of the braces may be necessary to achieve the proper angle for the main brackets. When correctly adjusted, the handle ends of the wheelbarrow frame should be about 28" apart.

To complete the frame, the wheel is then fitted into the front end with a suitable dowel axle, which can be made rigid to the frame by driving nails down through the frame and dowel on both sides of the wheel (see diagram in Fig. 8). The two rear legs, made of two pieces of 2"-by-4" lumber 18" long, are fastened to each side of the frame near the rear cross-brace, as shown in the diagram. If a barrel is to be used for the planter portion of the wheelbarrow, curved notches should be cut into the upper edges of the barrow frame (see diagram) to make a seat for the barrel. You will need to cut a rectangular hole out of the side of the barrel to convert it into a planter. First lay the barrel on its side and mark off the size of the hole. The measurements will depend on how large a planting area is desired. Then take a crosscut handsaw and hold it in a horizontal position across the arc of the barrel until it cuts through the top barrel stave. Now take a keyhole saw and finish the job with that. If you make your cuts evenly up to and through a stave at either end of the opening, you will not have to make any lengthwise cuts along the barrel because the staves will drop out as you cut

across them. The finished barrel can then be fastened to
the wheelbarrow frame with brass screws to complete
the planter.

Box Plant Holder

A box plant holder (Fig. 9) will add color to your patio

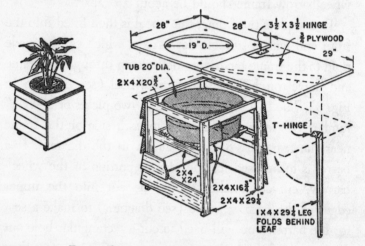

Fig. 9: Construction details for box plant holder.

and can also serve as extra table space when its dropleaf
is raised. A laundry tub filled with soil rests on a framework inside the box with a plywood top covering the metal
rim and handles. You can make the simple frame from
2″-by-4″ lumber stock. It is better to buy the tub before
building the shelf, so you can adjust the height as necessary. Build in the shelf for the tub before closing in the
sides with beveled lap siding. You can miter the siding
at the corners to make a neat joint or make the sides square

PLATE 7: With these "plant walkers" you can turn any tub, barrel or box planter into a portable unit.

PLATE 8: Hanging planters with staghorn fern add a luxuriant look to a modern doorway.

PLATE 9: A miniature planter box you can build yourself. (*Courtesy, California Redwood Association.*)

PHIL PALMER

PLATE 10: Spoon racks and napkin holders make very attractive planters.

PLATE 11: A planter bin covered with plastic paper made to resemble bricks enlivens this living room.

REYNOLDS, PHOTOGRAPHY INC.

PLATE 12: A window-box arrangement suitable for picture windows where baseboard radiators would

and use metal corners. Cut out the big center hole for the planter with a keyhole saw and smooth it with a rasp and sandpaper. Hinge the dropleaf to the underside of the top. For the leg on the dropleaf to be long enough to support the leaf when it is pulled out and still be able to fold up out of the way, mount the leg hinge near the edge of the leaf and at an angle as shown in the diagram.

THREE • Built-in Planters

Naturally, the ideal location for a built-in planter is in the home where it can be treated as an architectural element in the total design of the room. But it is misleading to associate stationary planters exclusively with interior decoration. There are many places outdoors in the garden or on the patio where a built-in unit can be used effectively.

As you will discover in this chapter, the built-in planter belongs as much to landscape design as to interior decoration.

BUILT-IN PLANTERS IN THE HOME

It is impossible in the confines of this book to give details for specific built-in planters because of the differences in room designs and layouts. The planters shown in this chapter are intended to stimulate your interest and imagination and to make you aware of the decorative possibilities of these units. However, if you want to get the best value from your interior planting enclosure, it must be designed with as much care as the room in which it is located. It should harmonize with the architectural background and decorative scheme of the room. It should provide enough drainage so that floor and wall finishes will not be damaged. And, of course, the planter must also meet the practical requirements of growing plants (see Chapter 5).

When determining the location of planters, you must examine your home interior with the same care and creative insight with which you planned the gardens, beds and borders in your landscape. You will find many locations suitable for raising house plants. The living, growing beauty of plants will enhance your rooms regardless of the season, but especially during the drab days of winter. Let us consider a few favorable locations for house plants and discuss how they may be blended into indoor planter gardens.

Picture-Window Planters

During the growing seasons of the year your picture window frames a colorful vision of loveliness. Heralding the return of spring, crocuses, daffodils, hyacinths and tulips leap into glorious bloom and gladden your heart with their masses of rainbow colors arrayed outside the window. And so, during the summer and autumn, your carefully planned display of choice blooms becomes a part of the warmth and loveliness of your room. However, during the winter months even the most artfully devised arrangement of trees, shrubs and evergreens cannot quite replace the riot of color you have become accustomed to seeing framed in the window.

What simpler solution can you think of than to plant a colorful or interesting "border" of house plants in front of your picture window, where they will add their bright beauty and interesting texture all year round. It is possible that you will find a table which can be used for this purpose. But more than likely the tables you find will be too short to extend across sufficient window area for a pleasing arrangement, too high and ungainly to look well when viewed from the inside or out, or too wide not to create a nuisance by cramping the living area.

The perfect solution is to build your own planter bin that will fit the area exactly. Fig. 10 shows a simple planter bin which can be built of 1″ redwood, cedar, cypress, clear pine or ¾″ plywood. The dimensions given can be varied to fit your own requirements. (The planting

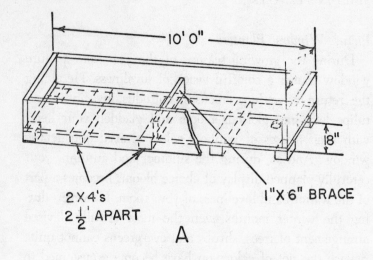

10' 0"

18"

2 X 4's
2 ½' APART

1"X 6" BRACE

A

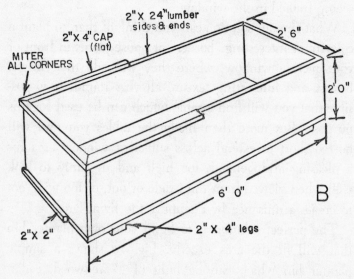

2"X 24"lumber
sides & ends

2"X 4" CAP
(flat)

MITER
ALL CORNERS

2' 6"

2' 0"

6' 0"

B

2"X 2"

2" X 4" legs

Fig. 10: Construction details for a simple wooden planter bin.

layout for this planter is illustrated in Chapter 5, Fig.
21.) This plant bin can be built with simple carpentry
tools usually found in the average household. The planter
bin in the illustration is 18″ deep, 2′ wide and 10′ long.
It was built with ¾″ by 18″ strips of exterior grade plywood. A false floor rests on a base of 2″-by-4″ braces
placed about 2½′ apart. A 1″-by-6″ brace located in the
center of the box keeps the sides from bulging. The floor
is sloped and calked like a boat so that surplus water will
run out only at the drainage holes in the lower end. A
piece of screen wire is placed over the drainage holes to
prevent the soil from falling through. An opening near
the floor allows just enough room for a pan to catch the
water. The inside of the planter may be waterproofed with
asphalt paint. The outside of the unit can be painted,
stained or wallpapered to blend with the decorative scheme
of the room. Or you could cover the bin with plastic
paper made to look like bricks (Plate 11) or fieldstone.
The simulated plastic material may be purchased at most
building-supply dealers. Tacks or adhesive tape will hold
it securely to the bin.

If you wish to eliminate the drip pan and the asphalt
paint, a waterproof liner can be installed in the planter
instead. The material for the liner can be copper-clad
building paper, thin aluminum, heavy waterproof paper
or plastic-coated waterproof paper. Take careful measurements of the inside of the box as shown in Fig. 11, Section A, for length (X), width (Y) and depth (Z). To
determine the amount of material needed, the inside

length (X) added to twice the depth (Z) will give you the overall length and the inside width (Y) plus twice the depth (Z) will give you the overall width. Cut a rectangle of the lining material to conform to these measure-

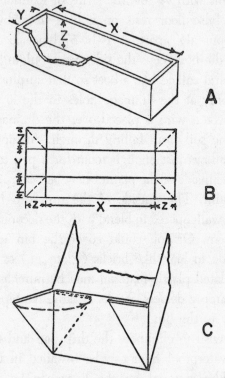

Fig. 11: How to measure and fold a waterproof liner.

ments. Next, draw lines on the material as shown in Fig. 11, Section B. With the waterproof side facing up, fold the material upward to make creases along both the vertical and horizontal lines. Then crease the corners along the diagonal lines as shown. Fold the corners first out and then back, parallel to the ends of the liner as shown in Fig. 11, Section C. Then place the liner in the planter bin. The pressure of the dirt will hold the flexible sides against the unit or if the unit is going to house potted plants set in moss or vermiculite, you can use a few tacks at the top to hold the liner in place.

If the picture window is too high for the unit to rest on the floor, the planter bin may be set on wooden or wrought-iron legs. These legs are available in a variety of styles at most hardware stores, in sizes ranging from 6" to 14" high. The legs should be attached to the 2"-by-4" supports not more than 4' apart to prevent sagging. If you use legs on the unit, a waterproof bin is a must.

In some picture-window arrangements, it may be desirable to use a window box setup like the one shown in Plate 12. This is especially true when there are baseboard radiators under the window and space is needed for the heat to escape. The interior window-box planter is constructed in the same manner as the exterior type that will be discussed later in the chapter. The indoor box is held on the wall by fastening it to the wall studs.

If it will not obstruct the view, you may wish to display plants in your picture window at a higher level. In this case, the planter bin may be supported on brass or wrought-iron brackets at any desired height. Before attempting to install an elevated unit, make sure that there is enough space in your window to use as many brackets

as you will need to prevent ugly sagging. The planter unit
need not, of course, extend entirely across the length of
the picture window. Where two glass wall areas meet at a
corner, it may be more desirable to use a triangular-shaped
planter than a longer unit along one wall.

If you are building or planning a new home, a planter
can be built-in into the room during the construction. The
window planter unit illustrated in Plate 13 is especially
adaptable to the basementless house. The masonry con-

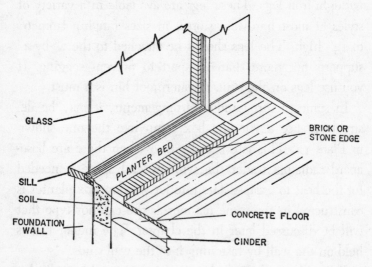

GLASS

BRICK OR
STONE EDGE

PLANTER BED

SILL

SOIL

CONCRETE FLOOR

FOUNDATION
WALL

CINDER

Fig. 12: Details for installation of picture-window planter shown in Plate 13.

struction (Fig. 12) requires a foundation that is carried
down to solid ground. Gravel and charcoal are essential
to keep the peat moss in good condition without having to
change it periodically.

Room Dividers

The modern-style home setting is again the inspiration for another dramatic location for an indoor planter. Many planters of the "bin" variety are extremely effective when used as dividers between various areas in the home.

In many newly designed homes the front door opens directly into the living room. To add an entrance "hall" that will not reduce the overall size of the living room, the simple low planter-divider sketched in Plate 14 is ideal. It can, of course, be modified to fit your particular requirements. The unit shown is essentially a wood frame made of 2"-by-2" lumber to which sheets of Fiberglas paneling have been attached. The frame is nailed to the beams in the ceiling and to the base and sides of the standard planter bin (see Fig. 10). This simple entrance divider will give you privacy but still allow complete passage of light. Plants can be placed on both sides of the screen paneling. Another version of the planter bin entrance divider is shown in Plate 16.

Planter-divider units may be used effectively in many of the other rooms of your home. The unit shown in Plate 15 would be fine between a dining room and living room. This unit also uses Fiberglas, but the paneling could just as well be hardwood plywood, hardboard or any other similar material which would fit the decorative scheme of your room. The space between the two screens can be filled with shelves for books or ornaments.

To install a planter-divider, you will need to locate the

beams in the ceiling to which you can fasten the top flanges on the short pieces of pipe that will support the unit. It would be easier to build the screens on the floor or in a workshop before they are put in place. Each frame is made of two short and two long pieces of 2"-by-2" lumber nailed together. Use wood screws to fasten the bottom flanges of the pipe sections to the top of the frames. Trim the flange edges to the width of the frame with a hacksaw. First drill holes in the crown of every third corrugation. Use ordinary wire nails on the frame, not finishing nails, and hammer only until the nails touch the material. Now lift the finished screens into position and screw the top flanges into the ceiling. With a level, check the position of the uprights. When they are level from floor to ceiling, toenail them to the floor. Coat the inner surfaces of the plywood with two coats of asphalt paint. (This step may be omitted if you use exterior-type plywood.) Then construct a waterproof liner for the planter box as previously described. To complete the planter-divider, finish the wood surfaces as desired.

Many smart indoor planter gardeners are discovering that a bin-type planter running the full length of the counter or bar which separates the kitchen and dining areas is most effective. This arrangement is a particularly cheerful addition to the home because it brings the joys of outdoor living into work areas where the busy housewife spends much of her time. Of course, if you do not have the necessary space for such a unit, you may try hanging your planter as shown in Plate 17. The plants in the suspended unit are illuminated by recessed fluorescent light tubes in the ceiling—a combination of daylight and white fluorescent tubes which supply about 1000 footcandles of light—enough "sunshine" for the sturdy foliage plants.

Room dividers also can be made of masonry materials like brick, stone or blocks. While masonry units are generally constructed when the house is being built, your local masonry contractor can do this job easily, inexpensively and without mess even in an old house. When building such planter units, be sure that only waterproof cement is used and that the inside walls and the bottom are given several coats of asphalt paint. It is also advisable to have some type of plant box liner provided for in the unit.

Other Interior Planter Ideas

These are only a few of the areas which may be beautified by an indoor planter. A simple planter such as the one shown in Plate 18 adds beauty to a fireplace. The kitchen and bathroom are also ideal spots for planters. The plants, too, like these locations since they thrive in the humidity created by the shower or bath and are so near a source of water that they are seldom allowed to get thirsty. Planters also can be built-in pieces of furniture as shown in Plate 19.

If you have an open stairwell you can make a little garden by the stairs in a metal (preferably copper) planter tray. If you are proficient in bending and soldering sheet metal you can easily make the tray to fit your requirements or a metal workshop will make one up to your

Fig. 13: Planter unit to use with an under-the-window radiator.

specifications for a very reasonable sum. The height of the tray should be from 3″ to 4″. After the tray is fastened in position on the floor, fill it with an inch or two of pebbles. The pots are then set down on the ground with a few larger stones scattered on top. Keep the tray filled with water just up to the bases of the pots. As the water evaporates the leaves will receive the needed moisture in the form of the humid air which rises around them.

There are endless ways to use planters in remodeling work. For instance, if your problem is concealing an under-the-window radiator and providing more storage space, the planter idea sketched in Fig. 13 could be very useful. Construction of this built-in unit is relatively simple (see Fig. 14) and could be done on the job without special tools. Stock lumber and plywood are used throughout. The

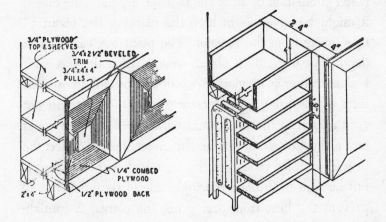

Fig. 14: Construction details for under-the-window radiator planter unit in Fig. 13.

doors are built of ½" plywood backing, with striated ¼"
plywood glued to the face. To achieve a contemporary
look, the striated plywood is quartered and set on in four
sections. This same quartered grain effect can be achieved
with walnut or mahogany veneer where a natural wood
finish is desired. The beveled strip applied to these doors
eliminates the usual jamb-facing on such units. The doors
are hinged at opposite ends of the cabinet so as to meet
in the center. This overlapped facing on the doors makes
them easier to fit into the cabinet. A simple grille for the
radiator is made from 1"-by-4" lumber. The grille strips
could be set on at an angle but would be equally satisfactory when placed flat, as shown in the illustration.
Notice that the detail drawing (Fig. 14) shows that the
toe space beneath this grille is left open in order to provide
better circulation of air to the radiator. By the same token,
it might be advisable to keep the planting box about 3"
to 4" away from the radiator. The plant box can vary in
depth, but 6" to 8" is about average. Line the box with
a planter liner as previously described. Insulate the undersides of the liner with asbestos so that the heat will not
get through to the plants and harm them. Or you could
tack a sheet of aluminum on the under shelf to deflect the
heat. A simpler version of this unit is shown in Plate 21,
but be sure to insulate the underside of the plant box to
prevent the heat from drying out the plants. A humidifying pan kept filled with water should be located somewhere in the planter bin unit.

As you can see, there is a permanent planter for almost every location in your house. Look over your rooms carefully and see just where you can use a planter to the best advantage. Then construct it following the general techniques described in this chapter. Once the planter is completed, you can select, arrange and plant it as described in Chapter 5.

BUILT-IN PLANTERS OUTDOORS

Exterior planters, like their indoor cousins, may be of either the stationary or portable variety. In the previous chapter we discussed the portable planter and its many exterior uses. The exterior built-in planter actually becomes a part of the structure of the house, patio or garden. Such a planter may range from a window box to a raised unit that runs the entire length of the house. Actually, any permanently located container that will hold a reasonable amount of good soil and provide good drainage will serve as a stationary planter. Properly proportioned and simply designed, a stationary planter can be used with almost any style of architecture and will provide a good home for most plants. To see what type is best suited for you, let us start our discussion with the raised-style planter. It is, of course, impossible to give exact plans or construction details in a book of this size since every house presents a totally different problem. But we will try to give an understanding of the tools and techniques involved with the hope that you will be inspired to design and build units to meet your particular specifications.

Raised Planters

Raised planter beds are becoming more and more popular in home landscaping, for several different reasons. First, they eliminate the aches and pains of gardening by raising the level of your garden beds so you do not have to bend over when planting, weeding and spraying. They also give you growing areas with excellent drainage to use where impervious rock or hardpan would prevent gardening under normal conditions. In other words, raised planters ensure early spring drainage and the drying off of the soil so it can be prepared and, if necessary, replanted earlier. The retaining walls of raised planters (which can be of concrete, stone, brick or durable wood) will keep out the hungry roots of nearby shrubs or trees which would otherwise compete with the plants for food and moisture. Soil can be prepared that will exactly fit the requirements of your plants. Grass and weed intruders are more easily controlled in a raised bed. Choice plants are also given an extra measure of protection from neighborhood dogs and other trespassers when the specimens are located in a raised bed. Unusual foliage and flowers are brought closer to eye level for the observer's greater enjoyment. If the walls are built wide enough, their copings will provide a welcome seat (and a drier one than the surrounding grass) when you want to work on the plants or just pause and rest. In addition, a raised planter is fairly easy to construct.

When planning your planter, study your house first. Remember that outdoor planters should become a definite part of the architectural structure of the house. From the landscape architect's point of view, foundation plants serve a three-fold purpose. They act as a screen, hiding the awkward corners where the house foundation meets the soil; they provide a tie-in between the house and garden; and frequently, when foliage plants are used, they are a backdrop for flowering shrubs. From an architectural standpoint, a large bare wall can be made infinitely more interesting by a raised masonry planter wall set along its base. From a distance, the masonry work, set about 2′ to 3′ from the wall, will give the illusion of being part of the house itself. The planter wall can be laid out in a straight line parallel to the wall of the house; or, for an often better effect, it can be laid in a free-form, curvilinear pattern. The planters can be made of various masonry materials, such as new or used brick, field stone, ashlar, flag strips, concrete blocks, etc. Choose the type that best complements your home.

To build a masonry planter, lay out the course you want it to follow on the ground and dig a trench 6″ to 19″ deep along this line, making it 3″ to 4″ wider than the masonry wall you are planning. Fill this trench with concrete to serve as a firm foundation for the plant wall. The concrete may be of the ready-to-mix type, or it can be mixed from 1 part cement, 3 parts sand and 5 parts gravel. The foundation (or footing) should extend below local frost penetration, which will vary for your area from 12″ to 36″. Your local building department will be glad to give you this information.

Once the footing is dry, lay the stones or bricks on it, using mortar and checking each masonry unit with a level to make sure it has been laid evenly. Again, ready-to-mix mortar may be used, or the mortar can be made with 1 part cement, 1/10 part lime and 3 parts sand. (Do not mix more than a bucketful of mortar at one time.) If the ground slopes, you will have to make a stepped foundation and step up the stones, bricks or blocks consecutively on this foundation to keep the mortar joint lines level and straight.

As the wall grows in height, back it up with generous applications of mortar plastered against the inside surface for added strength. When using irregularly shaped stones such as field stone, ashlar, etc., balance the pattern for eye appeal by scattering the larger stones evenly among the smaller ones. It is a good idea to provide pipes or tubes near the bottom of the unit to carry off the excess water. Once installed, remember to clean out these drainage tubes or "weep holes" with a piece of wire every now and then, for they tend to clog.

When the wall has reached the height you want, trim it off with a cap of some material such as flag strips or concrete. Before you fill the planter with top soil or peat moss, it would be a good idea to coat the surfaces of your

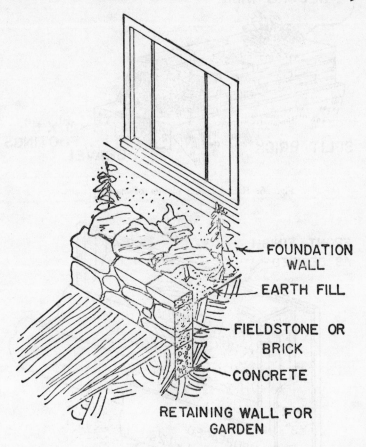

FOUNDATION WALL

EARTH FILL

FIELDSTONE OR BRICK

CONCRETE

RETAINING WALL FOR GARDEN

Fig. 15: Raised planter used as a retaining wall for garden.

house that will be underground with several applications of asphalt paint to protect them from rotting.

Masonry-raised planters of this type are not limited to use against the house. You can build them along a fence, as entranceway highlights (Fig. 15), or as retaining walls

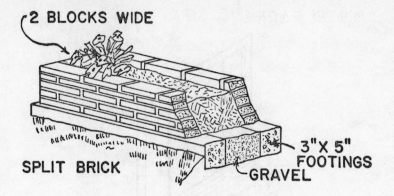

2 BLOCKS WIDE

3"X 5" FOOTINGS

SPLIT BRICK

GRAVEL

Fig. 16: Raised border planter of masonry units.

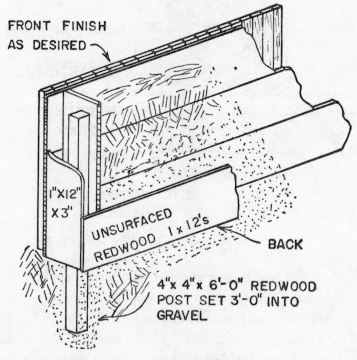

FRONT FINISH AS DESIRED

1"X12" X 3"

UNSURFACED REDWOOD 1 x 12's

BACK

4"x 4"x 6'-0" REDWOOD POST SET 3'-0" INTO GRAVEL

Fig. 17: Raised border planter of wood.

around the borders of a paved patio, porch terrace or walk. Circular or rectangular units can be built around garden lamp posts, mailbox bases or trees; they can also be used as corner accents or centerpieces for a patio or porch. Of course, where the border planter stands in the open away from a fence or wall, it will be necessary to construct two parallel masonry walls to complete it (see Fig. 16). Raised wood planters (Fig. 17) can be used in the same way as the masonry type. These are constructed in the same manner as the standard wooden planter box described earlier in this chapter.

It is possible to lay up a raised retaining wall planter following a so-called "dry wall" procedure. The term, dry wall, has nothing to do with the weather or the soil. It means a wall whose masonry units—preferably large field stones, mountain stones or quarried stones—are laid up without any mortar. Since no mortar is used, the stones can move slightly as the result of freezing and thawing without damage to the wall. Neither is a deep foundation or footing needed in this type of wall. Obviously, however, this kind of construction calls for careful work and some skill, so the wall will not, like those of Jericho, "come tumblin' down." But, on the other hand, a "dry wall" permits the growing of plants not only along the top, but also in front in the interstices between the stones (Fig. 18). Thus, such a unit becomes a wall-garden-planter.

Heavy flat stones of various sizes are laid with a slight tilt-back toward the planter bed and with a batter or slope-

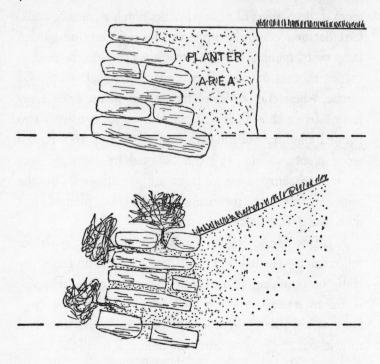

Fig. 18: Dry-wall planter.

back in the face of the wall. The slope-back should be from 1″ to 2″ for each vertical foot of the wall, depending on the flatness of the stones and the height of the wall. The greater the height, the larger the batter. Walls built with rounded stones need more batter than walls built with flat ones.

Place the heaviest stones at the base of the wall and patiently build the wall up stone by stone, laying each stone solidly and tamping the soil firmly back of the stones as the height of the wall grows. The smaller stones are placed near the top where they will form a level finish for the wall. Excess moisture in the planter bed will find its way out between the stones near the base of the wall, if drainage material has been placed in the bed at that level. In sections where hard freezing occurs, even the low dry-laid wall will benefit from a footing of concrete, extending 12″ to 18″ below the base of the wall.

A simple and attractive variation of the raised planter can be installed when a terrace or patio is being built by

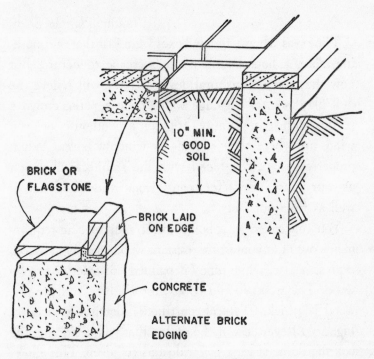

Fig. 19: Open patio-type planter.

leveling rectangular or round holes or pockets in the paving which can later be filled with growing plants (Fig. 19). Such pockets will give the illusion of plants growing out of the patio itself. With brick or flagstone patios, it is a simple matter to remove, or leave out, enough bricks or stones in a given area to provide an interesting free-form or symmetrically shaped pocket. To prevent the soil in these pockets from drying out, mix the soil with sand and gravel to provide good drainage and then enrich it with mulch and plant food.

Window Planter Boxes

Time was when window boxes were just that and nothing more, a housebound person's escape to nature. But now they are architectural devices. They will relieve the dull blankness of a garage wall, frame a patio, crown a portico with living beauty, brighten a penthouse, or even wind up where they started—as window boxes. When properly designed to blend with the architectural design of your house, they offer beauty from inside the home as well as from outside.

You can construct a box to meet your specific requirements out of any moisture-resistant wood such as redwood, cypress, cedar, white pine (if painted) or exterior fir plywood. The wood should be at least 1″ thick and the plywood ¾″ thick. (Typical construction details are given in Fig. 20.) Regardless of the design that you decide on, the box should be at least 10″ wide and 10″ deep. This allows

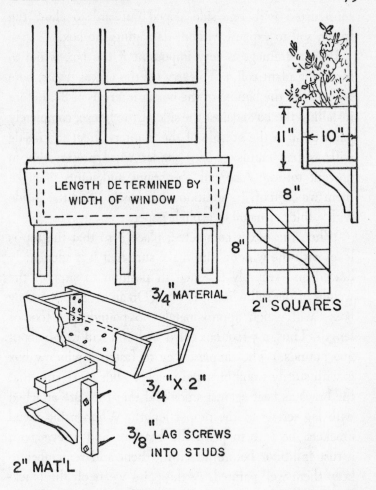

LENGTH DETERMINED BY
WIDTH OF WINDOW

11"   10"

8"

8"   2" SQUARES

3/4" MATERIAL

3/4" X 2"

3/8" LAG SCREWS
INTO STUDS

2" MAT'L

Fig. 20: Typical construction details of a window-box planter.

ample root depth for most window-box plants and sufficient room for making attractive plant arrangements. In
regions with severe winters, the window box should be

constructed with one side sloped outward to allow the frozen soil to expand without damaging the box.

Proper drainage is very important if the box is not to become a plant coffin. To carry off the excess water, bore ¾" holes in the bottom of the box at intervals of 8". Before installing the box against the side of the house, completely paint or stain the outside of the planter. Treat the inside with asphalt emulsion or a similar wood preservative to prevent rotting. Also calk the seams and joints to make them waterproof. In addition, it is wise to line the inside with a liner of metal or asphalt paper.

When the box is completed, place it so that the top is level with the window sill; make sure that it is adequately braced and securely fastened in position to support the weight of the soil when it is wet. (On an average, window boxes will weigh approximately 80 pounds per foot of length. Thus, a 5-foot box filled with soil will weigh about 400 pounds.) The simplest way to fasten a window box is with sturdy wood or metal brackets, but make sure that the brackets bear against studs and that they are attached with lag screws of the proper length. When using metal brackets, be sure to paint the brackets and screws with a rust inhibitor before attaching them and remember to keep them well painted. As the paint wears off the brackets, disagreeable stains will appear on the wall of your house and eventually the bracket and screws will rust through and let the box fall. It is a good idea to set the box an inch or so away from the wall of the house. This can be accomplished by using spacer cleats. After the box has been installed, fill the box up to 2″ from the top with a standard soil mixture. If you keep the plants in pots, of course, they may be surrounded with peat moss. Peat moss does not weigh as much as soil.

FOUR • What Will Grow in Your Planter?

What will grow in your planter? Any plant will thrive in a planter that can be grown in a pot or in open soil under similar physical conditions. In other words, almost all plants that can be successfully grown indoors or out, can also be grown in a stationary or portable planter. Some, however, due to their growing characteristics, are more adaptable for planter use than others.

In this chapter we will discuss the various species that are especially suitable for planter use, while in Chapters 5 and 7 we will analyze the actual selecting process of the plants you use. Plant selection should be undertaken with the same care you would exercise in selecting furniture for your home, because the success of your planter may be doomed to failure if good judgment is not used at this beginning point. One of the secrets of successful planter gardening is to use plants and flowers where they seem to belong naturally. It will only mean added expense and constant care if you plant colorful blooms in a shaded planter where they will not be at home. A happier (and more practical) solution is to use plants that will thrive in shade. Therefore, it is important to know the plant's characteristics and cultural requirements before making any selections.

FOLIAGE PLANTS

The foliage plants described here are the ones most generally used and the culture described is for an interior planter—either stationary or portable. These plants may be used outdoors during the summer months but since they are subject to frost, they must be taken indoors in the fall. The plants marked with an asterisk (*), may be placed in a light, frost-free, cool cellar or sun porch for winter storage.

The plants given here are arranged alphabetically by their botanical names; common names, when known, are included in parentheses. These plants are generally available from your local garden center, nurseryman and florist, or may be obtained from one of the sources listed in the Appendix. When ordering plants, be sure to use their botanical names to avoid any confusion about the actual species you want.

Aglaonema simplex (Chinese evergreen) has shiny, pointed, dark green leaves and grows as high as 3′ tall. Two other popular aglaonemas for planter use are *A. Robelinii*, a fine, robust plant with large, broad leathery leaves mottled with gray, and *A. costatum*, a small plant (6″ to 10″ high) with oval-shaped leaves with silver markings. All aglaonemas thrive in average soil, under poor light and in average room temperatures.

Alocasia amazonica, a glorified relative of elephant-ears and caladiums, is a very desirable planter plant because of its elegant appearance and liking for shade. It has beautiful dark, shiny ivy-green leaves veined with gray-white. This plant should be kept warm—never below 60 degrees—and the best potting medium is one with especially good drainage.

Araucaria excelsa (Norfolk Island pine) is that shamrock-green, feathery plant that florists use with cut flowers. It is said to be a member of the lily family but looks enough like a fern to please fern lovers and is much easier to grow. It prefers partial sun, average soil and average room temperature. This plant is an active climber and develops branches 2′ to 3′ long.

Asparagus sprengeri (emerald feather) is a fernlike plant from South Africa with sprays of long, feathery branches. It does well at ordinary room temperatures, in average soil mixtures and in partial sun. Its drooping stems grow 1′ to 3′ long.

Aspidistra elatior (cast-iron plant) is one of the toughest house plants, which will thrive almost anywhere, in any soil, and be able to stand shade almost indefinitely. It has fairly handsome, elliptic, broad green leaves and grows to heights of 3′. *A. elatior variegata* is a similar plant but its leaves are handsomely striped with creamy white.

Asplenium nidus (bird's-nest fern) is a true fern despite its unfernlike appearance, with long, glossy, light green uncut fronds (leaves) that grow to heights of 2′ or more. This very handsome East Indian plant develops a downy miniature bird's nest in its crown as it grows older. It prefers acid soils and can take shade and average temperatures, but needs good atmospheric humidity for best development. *A. bulbiferum* is a similar variety except that it has more graceful arching green fronds.

Aucuba japonica variegata (Japanese laurel) is a very colorful plant with bright green, glossy leaves, shaped somewhat like those of a rhododendron but with coarsely toothed edges toward the tips. The leaves are mottled in white or yellow. These evergreens require cold growing conditions under full or partial sunlight. While aucubas grow quite tall (over 5′) they are slow growers.

Begonia argenteo-guttata has olive-green leaves, freely spotted with white, and coarsely toothed. This plant will grow to heights of 3' in humus soil and when grown in full sun and at temperatures of 55 to 65 degrees.

Caladium bicolor has gorgeous heart-shaped leaves in various colors with dark veinings of red, silver or green and with margins of yellow, white or purple. These plants thrive in humus soil, in partial shade and at average room temperatures.

Carludovica palmata (Panama-hat plant) is a tall (up to 5') palmlike plant with many long-stemmed, hand-shaped leaves arising from ground level. It prefers sunny spots, a room temperature of 60 to 70 degrees and will do well in ordinary soil.

Caryota mitis (Burmese fish-tail palm) grows best in a partially shady location, under average room temperature and in a standard soil mixture. It has well-shaped palm leaves, branching out at its base and reaching lengths of 4' to 6'. *C. urens* (toddy palm) requires a similar culture but does not branch at the base.

*Chamaerops humilis (dwarf fan palm) is a compact fan-leaved palm-type plant that grows as tall as 5'. It prefers an east or west window, but a north window or even interior locations will do if the plant receives good light and an occasional shift into sunlight. Room temperatures of 55 to 65 degrees are considered best. The plant can be grown in average soil.

Chrysalidocarpus lutescens is a feather-leaved palm that is particularly beautiful because of the yellow color of its stems and leaf bases. It grows to heights of 3' or more in ordinary soil and in partial shade.

Citrus taitensis (Tahiti orange) has foliage that is excellent for a planter, but is wide-spreading and takes up considerable space. This plant needs a lot of sun and room temperatures of 55 to 65 degrees. Citrus plants of various kinds, including lemons, oranges, grapefruits and kumquats, are suitable for planters. The most popular varieties in this group are *C. mitis* (Calamondin orange), *C. Limonia* (lemon), *C. ponderosa* and *Fortunella japonica* (kumquat). To have fruit the following year, you will have to hand-pollinate these plants—which simply means transferring the pollen from one blossom to another.

Codiaeum variegatum (croton) in its many varieties is more bizarre than beautiful. Its evergreen leaves are very tough and variously shaped; they are variegated with yellow, scarlet, green, white and pink in all sorts of patterns and combinations. Actually, no two plants are alike and even on a single plant the colors will vary from leaf to leaf. In soil with good drainage, they grow to 3' or more under average room temperatures. They prefer bright sun—southern or southwestern exposure—but can stand some shade.

Coleus Blumei (painted nettle) is probably the best known and most highly colored of the coleuses. Its leaves are colored rich crimson, rose, maroon, green, yellow or orange, frequently with scalloped light-colored edges. The coleus forms small lilac or blue flowers, but they are not particularly attractive and should be pinched off to encourage a bushy habit of growth (it is a rather low plant) and so they will not detract from the leaves. These plants are tolerant of sun or shade, but the foliage colors will be deeper with sunlight. They do well in standard soil mixtures and at ordinary room temperatures.

Collinia elegans is an attractive, feathery-leaved palm that grows anywhere from 2′ to 8′ tall. But even when full grown, it does well in a 6″ to 8″ pot. (It likes to be moderately pot-bound.) It is very tough and hardy and is suitable for almost any interior planter.

*Cordyline australis (Ti tree) has numerous narrow green leaves, 1′ to 3′ long, that arch gracefully from a central stem and form a plant of great symmetry. Mature specimens attain a height of several feet but take many, many years to do this. This plant prefers ordinary soil and partial shade, but thrives best in a cool, frost-free location, 40 to 55 degrees.

Cyperus alternifolius (umbrella plant) is a graceful green plant with stems 2′ to 3′ tall, each topped by a feathery umbel of narrow, spreading and arching leaves. It does well at average room temperatures and in standard soil, but cannot tolerate much shade. Being a bog plant, it requires soil that is always wet. *C. alternifolius variegatus* has leaves striped with yellow.

Cyrtomium falcatum (holly fern) is a handsome stiff-foliaged, dark green fern that has fronds 1' to 2' long. Each glossy leaflet bears some resemblance to holly. The stems of the leaves are green, which distinguishes this plant from a similar fern, *Pellaea viridis*, which has dark brown leaf stalks.

Dieffenbachia picta is an erect, thick-stemmed plant with broad, paddle- or oval-shaped leaves generously spotted and blotched with creamy white. These plants like humus soil and bright light, but not direct sun for long periods. Several other species of dieffenbachia are suitable for planters; the best known are: *D. Hoffmanii, D. picta superba, D. Bowmannii, D. picta Robert Roehrsi, D. picta Jenmannii, D. Leonii, D. Bausei, D. Fasterii, D. seguine* (dumb cane) and *D. arvida.*

Dracaena fragrans has broad strap-shaped, drooping leaves that are 4" wide and 2' to 3' long, with a broad central band of yellow. Other popular dracaenas for planter use are: *D. deremensis Bausei,* green with a broad, tapering yellow center stripe; *D. deremensis Warneckii,* grayish-green leaves bordered with slender white stripes; *D. massangeana* (corn plant) long cornlike foliage with greenish-yellow stripe down the center; and *D. sanderiana,* gray-green foliage with broad cream margins. Some varieties, such as *D. godseffiana,* bear no resemblance to corn plants at all, having small, deep green, oval leaves profusely spotted with cream. The foliage of the varieties of *D. terminalis* has the long and narrow look of corn plants but the colors are mostly bright red. All dracaenas prefer partial shade, average soil conditions and standard room temperatures.

* *Euonymus japonicus* is an evergreen shrub that eventually attains large dimensions but is attractive as a small or medium-sized specimen in a planter. It has small white- or yellow-bordered green leaves. *E. japonicus aureo-variegatus* has small shiny green leaves variegated with creamy white. These plants do well in ordinary soil and partial shade, but need a cool temperature, 40 to 55 degrees.

* *Fatshedera Lizei* is a really tough foliage plant able to stand poor light, dry air, average soil and sudden changes in temperature. This cross between English ivy and fatsia combines the best features of both, ivylike leaves and a leathery glossy texture. The plant grows 2′ or more in height.

Fatsia japonica (aralia) can stand shade, dry air and poor conditions in general. As long as it is kept moderately well watered, it will continue to put forth its handsome, large, glossy-green, hand-shaped leaves. It will grow to 3′ tall at maturity.

Ficus benjamina exotica grows eventually into a tall tree but is very attractive in its immature state as a tub or planter-box plant. It has evergreen leaves that somewhat resemble in shape those of the peach tree. It grows well

in poor light, in ordinary soil and average room temperatures.

Ficus elastica (rubber plant) can stand heat, dryness
and lack of sun for months on end. Given half a chance,
however, it becomes a large, handsome plant (4′ tall and
up), well balanced and symmetrical. Its leaves are oval-
oblong and shiny green. There are several variegated
species which have the same characteristics but have leaves
variegated with cream, white and gray-green.

Ficus lyrata (fiddle-leaf plant) is an important-looking
and highly decorative plant. It has the same general habit
of growth as *F. elastica* (it is not quite as tough as its
cousin), but with bolder, larger leaves that are distinctly
fiddle-shaped, 10″ to 18″ long and dark green in color.

Howea forsteriana (flat palm) is a dark green feather-
leaved palm that can withstand poor light and other difficult growing conditions. Eventually, in average soil and
at ordinary room temperatures, it will grow several feet
in height, but it is slow-growing and is generally more
useful for planters in its small and medium stages of
growth. *H. belmoreana* (curly palm) is similar but has
leaves that are much more arching.

* *Laurus nobilis* (sweet bay) is an evergreen tree of the
shrub variety, suitable for planters if it is kept pruned.
It is easily grown in ordinary soil and under average sun
conditions, but needs a cool temperature.

Ligularia kaempferi aureo-maculata (leopard plant) is a
spreading, 1′ tall plant with round, green leaves conspicu-

ously mottled with yellow. *L. kaempferi argentea* is similar but has leaves marked with creamy white. It prefers bright, diffused light (not direct sun) and standard soil mixtures, but should be used only in planters where cool temperatures can be maintained.

* *Ligustrum japonicum,* usually used as privet, has handsome dark green leaves, 3″ to 4″ long that make it good for planters when properly pruned. (It may be pruned to any height.) It can be grown in partially shaded spots in ordinary soil. For best results the room temperature should be kept somewhere between 55 to 65 degrees. Other ligustrum species, such as *L. lucidum, L. lucidum aureomarginatum* and *L. excelsum superbum,* are also good for planter use.

Maranta leuconeura has green leaves with chocolate blotches on either side of the midribs. Given a humus soil mixture, partial shade and average temperature, this small plant (12″ to 18″ high) will give good results and provide an element of contrast in your planter.

Monstera deliciosa (Swiss-cheese plant) is a tall-growing tropical climber that is useful for planters in its small sizes when grown on a mossed stick, tree branch or piece of bark. Its large, rounded green leaves are cut at the margins and have conspicuous holes in them that add to their decorative appearance. It can withstand poor light, ordinary soil and average room temperatures well.

Musa nana is the dwarf banana tree (height 4′ to 6′). Its

leaves are green, 3′ to 4′ long and 2′ wide. This plant needs sun, good drainage and a 55 to 60 degree minimum temperature during all seasons.

Nephrolepis exaltata bostoniensis (Boston fern) produces more greenery with less care than almost any other foliage plant. There are many species—some small, some exceedingly large (up to about 5′), some lacy and frilled. A minimum temperature of 50 degrees suits them well and ordinary room temperatures are satisfactory. They thrive where illumination is quite poor, but prefer a humus soil.

Osmanthus fragrans (sweet olive) is a tall shrub useful for growing in a planter in its small as well as larger sizes. It has dark green, lance-shaped or oblong leaves. When planted in standard soil, it stands moderate shade but needs cool temperatures (40 to 55 degrees).

* *Osmanthus ilicifolius* (Chinese holly) is similar to English holly but its foliage is variegated with white. This plant likes the coolness of an unheated, closed-in porch (40 to 55 degrees), and partial shade. Under these conditions plus a humus soil, it will grow to heights of 4′ or more.

Pandanus veitchii (screw pine) is a beautiful foliage plant, approximately 2′ tall, with graceful sword-shaped leaves and a unique way of growing: On mature plants the leaves grow spirally, like threads on a screw, and are armed with rather formidable spines along their margins. The leaves are green, margined with silvery white. This plant does well in humus soil, average temperature and partial shade. There are other good screw pines for planter use including *P. Baptistii*, with blue-green leaves striped with yellow and without prickles; *P. Sanderi*, with yellow and green striped leaves with spines; and *P. utilis*, with blue-green leaves with red spines.

Peperomia sandersii (watermelon begonia) is grown in a planter for its low, decorative, silver-striped, bluish-green leaves; the flowers are insignificant. It grows best in humus soil, partial sun and at standard room temperatures.

Philodendron is the most commonly used and possibly the best-suited plant for use in planters. Philodendrons may be classified in three groups: vine or climbing; tree or arborescent; and rosette, self-heading or sessile. In general, philodendrons will thrive in average soil, standard room temperatures and shade. The climbers require the support of moss totem poles, pieces of bark or tree branches.

Fortunately, more and more of the 400 philodendron species, long known to botanists, are becoming available to the average gardener from South American jungles now easily reached by air. The variety in size, shape and growing habit of the many species makes it easy to choose an appropriate philodendron for almost every indoor planter. Some of the most popular species are:

P. Andreanum, a rather tender vine, with silky, dark green leaves and ivory veins.

P. cannifolium, a self-heading type that is small and

slow-growing, with light green leaves about a foot long on fat bulblike stems of the same length.

P. cruentum, a climber type with heart-shaped leaves, red in color on the underside and dark green above.

P. dubium, a vine type with deeply lobed, dark green leaves, having a slightly raised, lighter green midrib.

P. elegans, a slow-growing vine type with large, deeply lobed, finger-shaped leaves.

P. erubescens, a vine type with large leaves and stems of a reddish-copper color.

P. Friedrichsthalii, a vine type. Its dark green leaves have oblong holes in their margins like imported Swiss cheese. When any split or cut-leaf philodendron (and monstera) stops splitting, this is generally caused by lack of light, soggy soil or lack of fertilizer.

P. gloriosum, a rosette type with large, velvety, dark green leaves, ivory veins and a distinctive red margin.

P. hastatum, a vine type with large, arrow-shaped leaves. A beautiful variegated form of this species has appeared in some collections.

P. imbe is similar to *P. hastatum* in growth and leaf shape, but has dark red spots on the leaf stems and leaves with reddish-colored undersides.

P. lacerum, a vine type with lobed leaves rather wavy at the margins; a sturdy grower.

P. mandaianum, a vine type, slightly reddish in color.

P. mcneilianum, a tree type with large, wavy, lobed leaves. This is a new hybrid.

P. Melinonii, a self-heading type; wide, heart-shaped leaves on short stems give it a stocky appearance. It varies in height from 18″ to 4′.

P. micans, a vine type with small, silky, dark green leaves with a red sheen. It is an attractive hanging or moss-stick plant.

P. nobile, a rosette type with long, leathery, straplike leaves. It flowers easily.

P. oxycardium (*P. cordatum*), a vine type with heart-shaped leaves; often grown in water. It also appears in a variegated form.

P. panduraeforme, a vine type with large, fiddle-shaped, dark green leaves.

P. pittieri, a vine type with broad, heart-shaped leaves. It can withstand the dry conditions typical of apartment life.

P. radiatum, a vine type with deeply cut, almost star-shaped leaves of a deep green color. It needs more light than most species for good growth.

P. sanguineum, a vine type with arrowhead-shaped leaves, blood-red underneath.

P. Selloum, a tree type with large, bipinnate (doubly feathered), deeply lobed leaves. It is easily grown from seed.

P. sodiroi, a vine type, often with rosette habit, with heart-shaped leaves with silvery gray blotches and red stems.

P. squamiferum, a vine type with leaves having five deep lobes and leaf stems covered with bright red fuzz.

P. tripartitum, a vine type with large, trilobed leaves. This is a sturdy plant which can stand full sun almost all year.

P. verrucosum, a vine type with large, heart-shaped, forest-green velvet leaves, veined prominently with bright olive-green and colored salmon-purple on the underside. The red stems are covered with a green fuzz that is quite attractive.

P. wendlandii, a rosette type with long, straplike leaves.

Phoenix roebelenii is an attractive palm with feathery green foliage. It eventually grows quite tall but will maintain small or moderate dimensions for many years. It stands poor light, average soil and ordinary room temperatures. *P. loureiri* is another plant that grows under the same conditions and is good for planter use.

Pilea microphylla is a rapid-growing plant with light green, succulent foliage and fernlike branches. It should be kept in a partially sunny location where the temperature is average. A standard soil is fine for this plant.

Pittosporum tobira is a rounded shrub that eventually grows very large but is equally attractive when small. Its leaves are egg-shaped (the narrow end toward the stem), thick and leathery gray-green with white variegations. This plant will grow in a standard soil mixture but prefers sun and cool temperatures.

Podocarpus neriifolia is a tall (5′ and up), dark green, narrow-leaved, treelike plant. Its culture is the same as for *Pittosporum tobira.*

Pteris ensiformis Victoriae is one of the best and prettiest ferns suitable for planter use. It can stand a lot of shade and is much better adapted to the normally dry conditions of the average home than most ferns. This plant is very graceful, with leaves delicately variegated with silver. Like most ferns it prefers a humus soil.

Rhapis excelsa (lady palm) is a tall (5' or more), fan-leaved palm that forms dense clumps of slender, erect stems with green foliage. It prefers standard soil, partial shade and room temperatures between 55 and 65 degrees. *R. humilis* is a more slender plant but has similar uses.

Rohdea japonica marginata has leathery, strap-shaped, black-green leaves with white margins. It grows very slowly to heights between 2' and 4'. This plant grows well in shade, ordinary soil and at average temperature.

Sansevieria trifasciata (snake plant) has long, narrow, stiff, leathery green leaves striped with gray or with a yellow band on the margins. It will grow in almost any environment, under any conditions.

Saxifraga sarmentosa (strawberry geranium) has beautifully variegated leaves edged in pink and white. It prefers good light but not direct sun.

Schefflera actinophylla (Australian umbrella tree) is a stately, highly decorative foliage plant with large, hand-shaped leaves of a bright, glossy green that produce an exotic effect. It grows as high as 5' or more. This tree makes an excellent planter plant, since it requires little care and adapts easily to conditions in the average home. It is tolerant of poor light, sudden temperature changes, dry air and all other plant miseries.

Syngonium podophyllum has leaves that are a solid light chartreuse color. A whitish cast appears all over the mature plant. This climber is generally trained on bark or moss sticks. Or it can be trained to make a beautiful pyramid "tree" by planting several plants together and using a wire frame. By nipping off the growing tips you can make a veritable bush appear at each leaf node. This plant does well in a humus soil and under average room conditions. It grows luxuriantly in shade or interior locations.

FLOWERING PLANTS

Since most interior planters are used as permanent or year-round decoration, the foliage plants just described are generally more suitable for interior planters than the flowering varieties. Because of a necessary resting period, a flowering plant's beauty exists only while it is in bloom. However, a few flowering plants that have a long season of bloom can be used with (or substituted for) the foliage types in an interior planter when color is desired in the decorative scheme. Seasonal flowering material such as azaleas, poinsettias, bulbs and other plants received as gifts throughout the year can be counted on to give the planter a colorful lift now and then. During the Christmas season, for instance, a poinsettia or two will help to add to the festive appearance of the room. A few Dutch bulbs

BILL HEDRICH, HEDRICH-BLESSING

PLATE 13: Planter units can be installed during construction of a new house; this one requires a foundation carried down to solid ground.

Plate 14: Simple low planter-divider used with Fiberglas paneling.

Plate 15: Planter-divider between living room and dining room.

PLATE 16: Here a simple planter bin separates the dining area from the living room. (*Courtesy, Westinghouse Electric Corporation.*)

PLATE 17: An unusual planter arrangement illuminated by fluorescent light fixtures in the ceiling.

PLATE 18: Wall planters add a note of color to this plain white fireplace.

(hyacinths, tulips, narcissuses or daffodils), placed in the moss of the planter in December or January and kept moist, will provide color during the late winter and early spring.

In case you should want to put some of your foliage plants outdoors in the summer to rest and recuperate, you can keep your indoor planter attractive by using the most rugged of the foliage plants plus the African violets, begonias, and other summer-blooming flowering plants, including some garden annuals. The indoor collection may be augmented by tuberous-rooted begonias, fancy-leaved caladiums, achimenes, fuchsias and gloxinias. Flowering annuals and perennials can be used successfully in planters —both interior and exterior types.

Flowering plants are more acceptable in exterior planters than in the interior ones since the natural blossoming season of flowering plants is during the spring and summer months when exterior planters are in use. Their color is desirable, too, because it gives that extra dash to an all-green landscape and solid house color. Further information on this can be found in Chapter 7.

Most flowering plants (unless otherwise noted) require good sunlight, prefer ordinary room temperatures and will grow reasonably well in a standard or ordinary soil mixture. The most suitable household flowering plants for planter use are:

Abutilon hybridum (flowering maple)—Year-round use. Grows above 5'.

Acacia baileyana—Year-round use. Prefers 40–60 degree temperature.

Achimenes grandiflora

Anthurium scherzerianum

Ardisia crenulata—Year-round use. Prefers 40–60 degree temperature. May be stored for winter in frost-free cellar or sun porch.

Azaleas in variety—Prefer acid soil and 40–60 degree temperature. May be stored for winter in frost-free cellar or sun porch.

Begonia semperflorens—Year-round use.

Beloperone guttata (shrimp plant)—Prefers acid soil.

Bougainvillaea—Year-round use.

Bromelias in variety—Year-round use.

Browallia speciosa major—Year-round use.

Camellia japonica (the common camellia)—Prefers 40–60 degree temperature. May be stored for winter in frost-free cellar or sun porch.

Chorizema cordatum (flowering oak)—Year-round use.

Chrysanthemums in variety

Chrysanthemum frutescens (marguerite daisy)—Year-round use.

Clivia miniata (Kafir lily)

Crossandra undulaefolia—Year-round use.

Cyclamen indicum

Daphne odora—Year-round use. Grows above 5'. Prefers acid soil and 40–60 degree temperature. May be stored for winter in frost-free cellar or sun porch.

Euphorbia pulcherrima (poinsettia)

Euphorbia splendens (crown of thorns)

Freesias in variety

Gardenia jasminoides (Cape jasmine)—Year-round use.

Gerberia jamesonii (Transvaal daisy)

Heliotropium peruvianum (heliotrope)—Year-round use.

Hibiscus rosa-sinensis (rose of China)—Year-round use. Grows above 5'.

Hippeastrum hybrids (amaryllis)

Hydrangeas in variety

Impatiens holsti

Jasminum grandiflorum (Spanish jasmine)

Kalanchoe Blossfeldiana coccinea

Lantana camara

Myrtus communis (myrtle)—Prefers acid soil and 40–60 degree temperature.

Neomarica gracilis

Nerium oleander—Year-round use. Grows above 5'. Prefers 40–60 degree temperature. May be stored for winter in frost-free cellar or sun porch.

Pelargoniums (geraniums) in variety

Plumbago capensis

Polyantha and floribunda roses

Primula obconica (primrose)

Saintpaulia ionantha (African violet)

Sinningia speciosa (gloxinia)

Trachelospermum jasminoides (star jasmine)—Year-round use.

Zantedeschia (calla lily)

VINES AND GROUNDCOVERS

As you will discover in Chapters 5 and 7, there is a definite need in most planters for vines and groundcovers. In some cases they are used to fill in the bare spaces between pots on the surface of the planter or to trail over its edges. In other instances, vines can be trained on trellises to form attractive backgrounds for specimen plants. Some varieties like *Aristolochia elegans*, *Clerodendron thomsonae*, *Hoya carnosa*, *Plumbago capensis*, *Pelargonium peltatum*, *Solandra nitida*, *Tibouchina semidecandra* and *Vinca rosea* will also add color to your planter with their attractive blossoms. Most vines are also suitable for growing as trailers in hanging planters and window planters.

In general, the only chore vines and groundcovers call for, aside from watering and feeding, is diligent pinching back and training during their active growing season. Some cultural hints for tending the more popular vines and groundcovers used in planters are given here:

NAME	LIGHT	SOIL	ROOM TEMPERATURE IN °F.	
Aristolochia elegans (calico flower)	Partial shade	Standard	65-75	degrees
Calathea Vandenheckei	Partial shade	Humus	50-65	degrees
Chlorophytum elatum (spider plant)	Partial shade	Standard	65-75	degrees
Cissus antarctica (kangaroo vine)	Shade	Standard	50-65	degrees
Cissus capensis (evergreen grape)	Shade	Standard	65-75	degrees
Cissus discolor	Shade	Standard	65-75	degrees

NAME	LIGHT	SOIL	ROOM TEMPERATURE IN °F.
Cissus rhombifolia (grape ivy)	Partial shade	Standard	65–75 degrees
Clerodendron thomsonae (bag flower)	Partial shade	Standard	65–75 degrees
Cymbalaria muralis (Kenilworth ivy)	Partial shade	Standard	65–75 degrees
Davallia bullata (ball fern)	Shade	Standard	65–75 degrees
Episcia in variety	Partial shade	Good drainage	65–75 degrees
Fiscus pumila (creeping fig)	Shade	Standard	65–75 degrees
Hedera canariensis	Partial shade	Humus	50–65 degrees
Hedera helix (English ivy)	Partial shade	Humus	50–65 degrees
Hoya carnosa (wax plant)	Sun	Standard	65–75 degrees
Nepeta hederacea variegata (ground ivy)	Partial shade	Standard	65–75 degrees
Pelargonium peltatum (ivy geranium)	Sun	Standard	65–75 degrees
Pellionia Daveauana	Partial shade	Humus	65–75 degrees
Philodendron oxycardium	Shade	Standard	65–75 degrees
Plumbago capensis	Partial shade	Standard	65–75 degrees
Rubus reflexus pictus	Partial shade	Standard	50–65 degrees
Scindapsus aureus (pothos)	Partial shade	Standard	65–75 degrees
Senecio mikanioides (German ivy)	Partial shade	Standard	50–65 degrees
Solandra nitida	Partial shade	Standard	65–75 degrees
Syngonium podophyllum	Shade	Humus	65–75 degrees
Tibouchina semidecandra	Sun	Standard	65–75 degrees
Tradescantia fluminensis (wandering Jew)	Shade	Standard	65–75 degrees
Vinca major	Sun	Standard	65–75 degrees
Vinca rosea (periwinkle)	Sun	Standard	65–75 degrees
Zebrina pendula (wandering Jew)	Shade	Standard	65–75 degrees

FIVE • Selecting and Arranging Plants in an Interior Planter

Everyone will agree that flowers add charm to a room. Foliage plants, too, used dramatically and with imagination, can contribute not only color but life and vitality to any interior, whether it is simple or pretentious. No room ever looks stiff or cold when graced with properly selected plants. Such plants can be used in a variety of ways to brighten drab corners or to emphasize various pieces of furniture. Decorators are using plants in many ingenious ways to add distinction to modern interiors. Decorators do not think of plants as merely colorful or beautiful individual specimens but as integral parts of the decorative scheme like furniture, rugs and wall hangings. They use plants to balance a furniture grouping, screen an entrance, link indoor with outdoor greenery, or to divide a room.

SELECTING PLANTS

A wide range of plants are suitable for interior planters and great variety is possible in the shape and color of the leaves and flowers. But when selecting plants, your first consideration must be the location of the planter and the plant's cultural requirements, if your planter is to be successful.

Planter Location

There is no perfect place to locate a planter in the home because every spot presents at least one problem for the plants to overcome. For example, a location may have poor light, the temperature may be too high, or the air too dry. But, regardless of the difficulties, some plants will propagate and grow to maturity in almost any location. Those plants with tough, leathery leaves and stems are the most tolerant of adverse conditions. For example, such staunch foliage plants as the peperomias, sansevierias, dracaenas, dieffenbachias, etc., will grow under almost any conditions in the home. Because plants differ greatly in their ability to withstand unfavorable growing conditions, you must know not only the needs of the plants you plant but you must also select varieties that can survive the growing conditions found in the planter. To make a successful selection of material for your planter, you will have to know the following information about your plants:

1. What temperature is best for them?
2. Do they need a moist or a dry atmosphere?
3. How much light do they need?
4. Are there any special conditions necessary for growth?

The answers to these questions for specific plants can be found in Chapter 4.

Temperature

In general, temperatures between 55 and 70 degrees F. are considered best for house plants. However, particular plant requirements vary considerably. Some plants do well in a cool section of the house, while others need almost tropical heat.

In locating a planter, study the different temperatures found in the room. Temperatures in different parts of the same room may vary tremendously. Locations close to radiators or heating ducts should be avoided unless special care is exercised. But excessive heat is not all that you must guard against; cold can be just as harmful. Do not fool yourself that because a thermometer hanging on an inside wall indicates a comfortable 70 degrees F., plants in a planter close to a window in the same room are living in that temperature. When it is cold outdoors, the indoor temperature near the window may be 15 to 20 degrees lower than the temperature in other parts of the room. The only sure way of determining the exact temperature prevailing where you plan to locate your planter, is to put a thermometer at that spot and watch it at different times of the day and night over a period of several days. The results may surprise you.

If you keep your plants near a window or glassed-in area, be sure to protect them at night, if the temperature is expected to drop suddenly. If you do not, they may be nipped by the cold or even partly frozen. This is most likely to happen at night when temperatures drop. You can prevent such damage by pulling down the window shades or closing the draperies. On very cold nights or during cold spells, put several thicknesses of newspaper or a piece of cardboard as insulation between the glass area and the plants. Low temperatures curtail growth and often cause the foliage to turn yellow and the leaves to drop off, beginning with those lower-most on the stems. Some plants, however, thrive best in colder rooms.

Excessive heat, especially if accompanied by too much shade, can cause plants to become spindly and weak; their stems lengthen unduly and the leaves are spaced far apart on the stem. Solid glass windows in full sun become very hot and often burn the soft growth close to them. Therefore, it is a good idea to set plants back approximately 3′ from the window if it is not screened by blinds or thin draperies.

Humidity

Houses are designed for people, not plants. For the most part, the houses we live in are too dry during the heating season. In a greenhouse the relative humidity is usually 60 per cent or over, but in the average home it seldom exceeds 30 per cent, except in the kitchen, bath or laundry. So when certain plants are moved from the moist atmosphere of a greenhouse, or even from the garden, into the dry air of a super-heated house, it is not surprising that leaves curl up, flower buds drop off and finally the plants collapse. This is due to the fact that dry air draws the moisture from the foliage faster than the roots can replace it.

There are several ways to increase the moisture in the air. During winter, the water reservoirs on hot-air furnaces should be kept filled. Pans of water can be placed on radiators when the heat is on to insure rapid evaporation. The peat moss, sphagnum moss, vermiculite or gravel in the planter will also help by preventing the soil in the pots from drying out too rapidly and by raising the humidity around the leaves where it is needed most. Humidifying pans hung near or placed in the planter will help, too.

To check evaporation on the plant itself, hand syringe the leaves daily with cool water during dry spells, and at least once a week at other times. There is one caution to observe here. Use a very fine, misty spray and do not prolong the application. Overwatering of foliage plants is just as bad for them as getting too little water. It is hu-

midity around the foliage that you want, not a continu-
ously soaking-wet soil. (Do not spray gloxinias or African
violets, as water on their leaves tends to cause yellow spots
and mottling, especially if the plants are exposed to direct
sunlight while still wet.) Also remember to keep the
leaves clean.

Groups of plants in a planter have an advantage over
single house plants as far as humidity is concerned. The
foliage of the plants gives off moisture; so does the damp
soil in the pot. If one plant does not have enough moisture
it will be helped by the humidity given off by its neigh-
bors. In modern homes equipped with air conditioning,
humidity control is not such a difficult matter and you can
create a better environment for your plants.

Light

All plants need light, but in different intensities and in
different exposure times. The rate of growth and the length
of time the plant remains in good condition in the home is
largely dependent upon the intensity of the light it receives, for light is a source of energy for the production of
plant food. For example, flowering plants usually need
at least three hours of sun every day, so do not place them
in shady planters or they will not bloom at all. Most foliage
plants differ in their light requirements. For instance, Chinese evergreens (Aglaonema), *Philodendron panduraeforme* and velvet leaf (*Philodendron micans*) all require
comparatively little light and so may be placed in planters
in the darker parts of a room. On the other hand, pepero-

mias, green and variegated, as well as *Philodendron pertusum*, sansevierias, Nephthytis and pothos will do better near windows but not in direct sunlight. Dieffenbachias and dracaenas thrive well under intermediate light conditions. As a consequence, your choice of plants for your planter should be governed in large part by the amount of light your house can give them.

In the home, three intensities of light are available: (1) *full sun* part of the day, which is best for nearly all the flowering plants; (2) *bright light* or *partial sun*, which is just out of the sun or in the unshaded north window, suitable for plants that flower for a short time and for most foliage plants; (3) *shade*, which is light of enough intensity to read by most of the day and is suitable for many foliage plants. (See Chapter 4 for light requirements for individual plants.) When considering light requirements for planter plants, remember that light in cities is often more subdued than country light because of the smoke and dust particles in the air. Light indoors is much less intense than outdoors, and light rapidly diminishes as one moves away from a window. Curtains and drapes cut down light considerably.

All window planters are not suitable for the same types of plants. The key to successful planter gardening is wise selection of plants to suit the exposure. For example, an east window is ideal for vines such as *Cissus rhombifolia, Cymbalaria muralis, Hedera canariensis, Hedera Helix, Plumbago capensis, Scindapsus aureus* and *Vinca major*.

The same exposure is favorable for growing begonias, fuchsias and foliage plants such as the Ti tree (*Cordyline australis*), dieffenbachias, dracaenas, *Pittosporum tobiras* and similar kinds of subtropical or temperate species.

A south window provides almost identical growing conditions for house plants as an east window. However, in the months from June to September, the full, direct sun is extremely strong and will burn the foliage of plants not suited to it. A south window planter is excellent for cacti and succulents. Most of the sun-loving plants described in Chapter 4 grow well in a south window, and it is also a superior location for most flowering plants.

West and north window planters provide little or no direct sunlight and certainly not enough for sun-loving species. But the diffused light of western and northern exposures is perfect for plants which normally grow in the shade of big trees or on west or north slopes outdoors. A west window planter, for example, is fine for all varieties of African violets. Most philodendrons, dieffenbachias, caladiums, dracaenas and ligularias also appreciate the partial shade or diffused light of a west window.

Most of the plants suitable for a west-window location will also do well in a north window planter. However, there are some plants that seem to prefer the sunless (diffused) light of a northern exposure. Among these are a variety of tender tropical foliage plants including the *Alocasia amazonicas*, *Maranta leuconeuras*, *Monstera deliciosas*, *Scheffera actinophyllas*, most philodendrons and the tender bromeliads such as the guzmanias and vriesias.

These plants will produce rich foliage in diffused light, whereas sunlight will discolor their leaves. Also recommended for northern locations are most ferns and plants described previously as being able to tolerate poor light. Plants in north and west window planters should be located so that they receive the maximum amount of light available. If the plants are placed too far away from the window, they will reach out for the light and become straggly. Regardless of where a plant is located, it should be moved a quarter turn regularly, lest in reaching for the light it should grow lopsided.

Artificial light may be used with some plants instead of, or in addition to, natural sunlight. Numerous plants actually perform better under fluorescent light or ordinary incandescent bulbs than under natural light. Using artificial light allows you to put planters in dark hallways, stairways, basement recreation rooms, and other places where plants would not normally grow.

The most practical artificial light for encouraging house plants is that of the ordinary 60- to 250-watt incandescent bulb or the fluorescent tube. Reflectors of any kind greatly increase the efficiency of the light source. To be effective, supplemental artificial lighting should continue or lengthen the natural daylight span. Artificial light applied for a few hours in the middle of the night does not seem to produce comparable effects. For once, the best way is the easiest—simply illuminate your plants when you would normally light the room for the evening hours. You can also use electric light on cloudy days to make up for the loss of natural light; for this purpose, an intensity of 50 to 100 footcandles is suitable. If you use floodlights or spotlights on your planter you can create dramatic pictures at night. Automatic control switches are available which will turn on and turn off the light systems. Thus, by using electricity and imagination, you can locate your plants wherever they will look best, instead of always putting them in your one sunny window, where they soon turn their backs on you to look outdoors.

The Lamp Division of the Westinghouse Electric Corporation has experimented with the effects of supplemental artificial lighting on foliage plants and has discovered that the following varieties show the best results: *Agalonema simplex, Araucaria excelsa, Aspidistra elatior, Aucuba japonica, Cyrtomium falcatum, Dieffenbachia picta, Dracaena deremensis, Fatshedera Lizei, Ficus elastica, Hedra Helix, Nephrolepis exaltata bostoniensis, Peperomia sandersii*, varieties of philodendron, *Pilea microphylla, Sansevieria trifasciata, Schefflera actinophylla, Scindapsus aureus, Syngonium podophyllum* and *Zebrina pendula*. For further information on growing plants under artificial light, you can write to the General Electric Company, Nela Park, Cleveland 12, Ohio; Sylvania Electric Products, Inc., 500 Fifth Avenue, New York 18, New York; or Westinghouse Electric Corporation, Lamp Division, Bloomfield, New Jersey. You may also find it helpful to read a book like Peggie Schulz's *Growing Plants Under Artificial Light*. Another good idea is to consult your electrician or nearest light and power company.

Ventilation

Fresh air is as important for plants as humidity. One word of caution, however: do not set plants where an open window or door will admit wind and cause drafts and sudden chill. It is better to open a window in an adjoining room, or to use ventilators or screens to prevent drafts. When locating a planter in an entranceway, be sure to place it so that it will not be in a direct draft. A simple screen arrangement or a change in the direction of the door will correct this difficulty.

The minute amounts of artificial gas that escape into the air (sometimes from faulty pilots, sometimes while lighting stove burners) may kill tender plants in a very short time. The only way to minimize the effects of escaping gas is to keep the stove in order and provide ample ventilation.

Select plants for your planters according to the amount of time you can spare to care for them. Even if you have only ten minutes a week, you can have a splash of growing green in your house. No matter how much or how little care you give, it must be on a regular schedule. (See Chapter 6.) To be sure, the plants in your planter have their little characteristic quirks that require some extra attention, but they can do something for your room that expensive rugs, beautiful curtains and ornaments never can.

ARRANGING PLANTS

Choosing the proper plants for your interior planter can present you with an interesting and endless challenge.

Even if you are one of those who has flinched from flower arrangements because they have become hackneyed, you can still try new, wonderfully varied compositions with living plants in a planter by playing one foliage form against another, scaling plants to each other and to their locations and trying all kinds of things that cannot be done with cut flowers because, once cut, they cannot be changed.

When selecting plants for your planter, you must be an interior decorator and very carefully study the room in which they are to live. You must decide whether to grow plants with upright foliage to heighten a long, low ceiling or whether you want feathery foliage to soften flat white walls, or whether you want sharp splashes of color or pastels in a quiet corner.

While there are no set rules for grouping plants in a planter, there are certain principles that you should keep in mind that will help you create interesting combinations. First, select plants with enough difference in color and foliage texture to create a definite contrast. For example, the large, shiny green leaves of *Ficus elastica, Fatsia japonica* and *Schefflera actinophylla* complement, and are complemented by the smaller dark green foliage of *Cyrtomium falcatum* and *Osmanthus fragrans,* or the light green, thinner texture of *Aglaonema simplex* and *Begonia argenteo-guttata* or the flat, fernlike foliage of *Nephrolepis exaltata bostoniensis* and *Asparagus sprengeri.*

The plant layout shown in Fig. 21 for the 10'-by-2' window planter detailed in Chapter 3 illustrates how in-

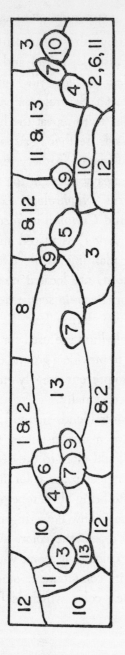

PLANTING KEY

1. *Syngonium podophyllum*
2. *Begonia semperflorens*
3. *Cissus rhombifolia*
4. *Ficus elastica rubra*
5. *Ficus lyrata*
6. *Zebrina pendula*
7. *Aucuba japonica variegata*
8. *Asparagus sprengeri*
9. *Small Fatsia japonica*
10. *Large Fatsia japonica*
11. *Crytomium falcatum*
12. *Pilea microphylla*
13. *Nephrolepis exaltata bostoniensis*

Fig. 21: Planting plan for window planter.

terest and charm can be obtained by using contrasting texture and color. Large aralias (*Fatsia japonica*) and Australian umbrella trees (*Schefflera actinophylla*) give a substantial background to the planter. Several small aralias are used near the ends of the planter to repeat the heavy, tropical-looking foliage. Emerald feather (*Asparagus sprengeri*), with lighter green foliage of feathery texture, forms the transition between the heavy leaves of the aralia and the finer foliage of the ferns—*Nephrolepis exaltata bostoniensis, Pilea microphylla* and *Crytomium falcatum*. A large fiddle-leaf plant (*Ficus lyrata*) is placed slightly off-center to add height to the planting, while two red rubber plants (*Ficus elastica rubra*) are located near the ends of the unit to add leaf color. *Begonia semperflorens*, grape ivy (*Cissus rhombifolia*), wandering Jew (*Zebrina pendula*) and *Syngonium podophyllum* are used for their color and contrasting foliage and to provide a ground cover. To keep the plants compact and to prevent straggly growth, pinch out undesirable sections occasionally.

While the green of foliage plants blends naturally into any decorative scheme, there are many instances when flowering plants in a planter will add more to the décor if they are chosen to pick up or repeat some color in the room. For example, if you want to bring out a tone of yellow in your curtains, then choose yellow flowering plants for your planter in the room to repeat the color. Where blue is to be the predominating color in a room, you can increase its intensity by using its complement, orange—not bright orange, but the peach color which is found in some begonias and patience plants. But, when using flowering plants in a planter, be careful not to select blossoms that will conflict with the room's furnishings. For instance, where tones and tints of red are dominant, do not choose flowers with a reddish-purple or magenta cast.

Recently I visited a friend's home where a remodernization job had just been completed in the kitchen. Between the dining and cooking area, a narrow planter was installed containing *Plumbago capensis*, whose sky-blue flowers exactly repeated the pale blue laminated plastic counter tops in the kitchen. Because of the plant's rampant growth, stakes were placed at intervals in the planter so that the vine formed a most effective screen. This planter unit was located near a window, where otherwise there would have been no flowers. But this same idea could have been used in a shady location with foliage plants or vines that prefer little sunlight.

You can, of course, brighten planters that do not receive direct sun with pots of flowering plants that can be replaced from time to time to maintain continuous bloom. The pots will be easier to remove and replace when their flowers drop if you group them together in small areas instead of scattering them all over the planter. You can get as much as three to five weeks of bloom from potted azaleas, geraniums and chrysanthemums if they are not in direct sunlight. They do need sun to bloom but, once open, they will last longer in artificial light.

Differing growth habits provide another point of contrast. The light, open form of certain palms such as *Howea*

forsteriana, Caryota mitis or *Carludovica palmata* may be
accentuated by the solid, compact form of others like
*Cordyline australis, Cyperus alternifolius, Euonymus ja-
ponicus* or *Laurus nobilis.* Or, sometimes, you may prefer
to carry the same quality throughout by using both low
and tall plants of similar texture and character. Or, you
may decide that the differing growth habits of plants of
the same species, such as philodendrons, prove most interesting.

Many of the planter arrangements in this book demon-
strate the value of grouping plants in three major divisions
according to height. The lowest plants in the grouping
serve as a groundcover and as a softening influence
around the edge of the planter. The latter effect is very
important in units that are raised well off the floor since
those plants (generally vines) which hang over the edges
will help to tie the planters to their bases. The medium-
high plants mask the bare stems of the tallest members of
the group and relate them to the groundcover. The tallest
members of the group give height to the entire unit as well
as to the room in which the planter is located. The purpose
of the planter also influences the selection of plants and
their arrangement. For example, most purely decorative
groupings generally consist of one large plant, three to five
medium-sized plants and several fillers or ground-cover
plants. But, where a planter is to be used as a room divider
or screen, tall plants should play the dominant role in the
arrangement.

Plants in a large window planter must be arranged to

form a pleasing appearance from the inside and at the same time to frame, not block, the view into the yard. Tall-growing plants are placed toward the back and sides of the planter, with the medium- and low-growing specimens in the center and at the front edges. In the case of a large window area, 10′ or more, a tall plant may be placed in the center to break up the length of the area. Upright plants are well suited for softening rectilinear lines and also for embellishing an interior wall of glass, brick or wood. Variety in plant and foliage forms prevents the transition from low- to tall-growing plants from becoming so even as to appear monotonous. Any arrangement that begins to resemble a counter where plants are displayed for sale should be suspect, for too much emphasis is being placed on individual plants. Group the plants without crowding to gain the best effect in the planter and remember that the plants will take up more space as they grow.

Planters often can solve your window-decorating problems for you. Perhaps you have a window where it is difficult to hang curtains. A friend of mine has a huge rounded window in her upper hall where she has used this effective treatment. At 10″ intervals over the top and around both sides, she has placed small white wrought-iron planter units containing trailing Spider plants (*Chlorophytum elatum*). While there is nothing unusual about the plants themselves, their use in a large grouping presents a charming picture around the window.

Frequently, it is possible to tie an interior and exterior planter together through a large modern window. Ferns, philodendron and ivy can be used indoors and out, pandanus and dracaena indoors and hosta outdoors to strengthen the continuity of the two planters. Fibrous-rooted and tuberous-rooted begonias are excellent plants to use to create a link between interior and exterior planters. Since growing conditions are so dissimilar between the two areas, it is seldom wise to duplicate the plantings on both sides of the glass. It is enough that a number of the same plants, or plants of the same variety, are used in both planters. Many of the hardy broad-leaved evergreen shrubs, such as andromeda, azaleas, laurel and rhododendron are frequently used as background for the outdoor portion of the planting, while the various aglaonema, dieffenbachia, monstera and philodendrons create a similar background effect indoors. When selecting plants for your planter, attempt to choose plants that have similar requirements—water, light, soil, temperature and humidity. This makes maintenance and care of the planter much easier. Such requirements as well as plant characteristics are discussed in the previous chapter.

INSTALLING PLANTS IN THE PLANTER

Plants in a planter may be grown in open soil, in pots placed on top of a layer of pebbles, or in pots set in moss (peat or sphagnum) or vermiculite. The last-named arrangement is usually considered best since it allows you to control root growth and humidity and yet gives the appearance of plants growing in the open. Another advantage in this method is that the plants can be changed easily by removing the pots and replacing them with plants in peak condition of full bloom.

To grow plants in pots set in a moss or vermiculite filler, first arrange the pots in the planter so they are level with each other. This can be done by placing the shorter pots on concrete blocks or pieces of wood to raise them until all the rims of the pots are at the same height from the base of the planter. For the best effect, the rims should be approximately an inch below the top edge of the planter. Place the pots in the desired arrangement and fill the planter with fine builder's sand or cinders until the tallest block or piece of wood is covered. Scatter a little charcoal over the sand or cinders to prevent it from turning sour. Then fill in the space around the pots to level with or slightly below their rims with a water-holding humus, preferably peat moss or sphagnum moss or vermiculite. About every other month each plant should be turned slightly in the moss or vermiculite. This will prevent the anchoring roots from taking hold through the drainage holes and also facilitate the development of shapely plants that do not lean more in one direction than the other. During the year it may be necessary to add a little moss to keep it level with the tops of the pots, since the moss has a tendency to settle. About every six months, loosen the moss or vermiculite with a hand fork or cultivator. A little charcoal mixed into the moss or vermiculite will help to keep it from souring. Avoid regular spacing in rows in favor of naturalistic grouping of plants as they might be found growing wild.

For the shallow-type planter, pots may be placed directly on an inch or two of pebbles, vermiculite or cinders. While this setup has some moisture-holding properties and allows movability of plants, it does not have the beauty of the previously mentioned plan since the pots are exposed. Using glazed pots will overcome this difficulty to some degree.

Growing plants in open soil in a built-in or stationary planter is not recommended since with this arrangement there is no way to control root growth, prevent insect or disease damage, or provide for summer care.

Staking and Tying

Since many plants in a planter are tall, some method of supporting them is necessary. The plant supports should be as inconspicuous as possible. This does not mean, however, that the supports should be so frail that they are not adequate for the job. When you look at the plants in a planter, you should not be conscious of the artificial supports.

Philodendrons and other aerial-rooting climbers grow well when climbing on a peat-moss or sphagnum-moss totem pole. To make such a pole, lay a wood stick of the desired height on a layer of peat moss laid out on a piece of paper. Roll the moss around the stick; it is easier to start the process by turning the paper up with the stick. When the moss is well started let the paper drop back and continue rolling the stick until the remainder of the moss is wrapped around it. Then bind the moss securely in place with copper wire. Insert the sharp bare end of the stick in the soil. It will be necessary to tie the plant to the stick at first to give it a start. It is better, of course, to put the supports in at potting time, but if you are careful to anchor the base of the plant firmly, you will be able to insert the supports later when they are required. The moss should be kept moist until the aerial roots have attached themselves to the support.

Another good totem-pole support can be made by forming a slender cylinder of ¼"-square wire mesh or hardware cloth. Roll the wire mesh (10" strip is a good size) into a cylinder, overlapping the edges about three-fourths of an inch. Then fasten the roll together at 6" intervals with short strands of wire and cut off the surplus wire or fold it into the cylinder. To steady the pole and help brace it, push small sticks through the mesh at the bottom of the cylinder, extending out approximately 5" on each side. Flat sticks give the best brace and are easy to insert.

After placing the totem pole in the planter, you are ready to fill the center cavity with a mixture of moist peat moss and vermiculite in equal parts. (Also mix in some pieces of charcoal.) Soak the peat moss in advance, if possible, and use a paper funnel to make filling the cylinder faster and neater. After filling the pole one-third full, push down the peat-vermiculite filler with a broom handle until it is packed tightly. Continue to fill and pack until the pole is full. To keep the pole moist, push a small pot into the cylinder, flush with the top. When the flower pot is filled with water, it will seep into the pole. If the pole is kept moist, the roots will grow into it and the vines will grow faster. You can add plant food through the pot, too, when necessary.

A slab of rough bark, such as redwood or cedar, or pieces of virgin cork fastened to wooden stakes may also be used to support aerial-rooting plants. These materials are generally available through garden-supply dealers. Spray the bark or cork occasionally with water to give the roots a good start.

Bamboo poles or canes are also satisfactory stakes to use for many plants. If stained green, they will be less conspicuous. One or two, or more, poles may be needed, depending on the size and shape of the plant. When inserting the pole try not to damage the root system. In some locations strings or wires stretched taut between screw eyes or nails may suffice to support light twining vines.

Neat tying is just as important as neat staking. Use soft raffia, darning wool or soft string of an inconspicuous color. Encircle the tying material around the stake two or three times at a point slightly higher than where the material is to be tied around the stem. Twist the strands a couple of times around both the stake and the stem to make them appear as one rather than two units. Tie with a square knot against the stem, not against the stake. Do not tie too tightly—allow room for growth. Also do not bunch the stems together. And try to hide the stakes as much as possible by tying the shoots over them. When staking and tying, try to keep the plants as natural-looking as possible.

To train vines on a totem pole, twist them to grow in a spiral around the pole. Do not train the shoots to climb straight up the pole, or the base will look bare. When using a wire mesh pole, fasten the vines to the pole with hairpins. Pins thrust into the pole at a steep angle will hold best. Use the largest available size so that the pins will not pinch the stems.

SIX • Special Care for Indoor Plants

A beautiful planter can be very rewarding. As I previously discussed, a planter will add interest to any interior arrangement. But only healthy plants are decorative in a planter and only a decorative planter is worth having. To keep your plants growing and flourishing beautifully, care is required. This includes watering, feeding, cleaning and constantly guarding against insects and diseases.

WATERING

Watering is one of the most misunderstood and improperly handled chores connected with growing plants in a planter. House plants can tolerate neither a too dry nor a too wet, soggy soil. If there is too little water, the plants will soon wilt. While drying-out seldom causes damage unless it occurs too frequently, the reverse—too much water—can be very serious. Generally the first symptom of too much water is that the lower leaves begin to drop. While new leaves may appear on the top, the overwatered plant becomes leggy and bare at the base. If you suspect that a plant may be waterlogged, tap it out of the pot and look at the roots. Healthy root tips should be white. But if they are brown, repot the plant in the proper soil mixture and water it less frequently in the future.

A safe rule-of-thumb is to water plants when the surface soil in the pots is light in color, feels dry and crumbles loosely between your fingers. The length of time between watering depends upon several factors including the kind of plant, the character of the soil, the condition of the roots, the stage of growth, the size of the plant in relation to the pot and such variable environmental factors as humidity, temperature and light. In general, the larger the leaf area, the more frequently a plant needs to be watered. Remember that since these factors may vary with different plants in the same planter, each one should be watered individually. In other words, do not water all the plants in your planter when you notice that one is thirsty. Treat each plant individually.

When a plant requires water, be sure to give it plenty, enough to saturate all the soil, not an insignificant dribble that wets only the surface. The excess water will run out the drainage hole in the pot into the sand or fine gravel at the bottom of the planter. This sand or gravel, along with the peat moss or sphagnum moss set around the pot, will act as a reservoir for excess water. But be sure that you are watering the entire ball of soil around the plant and not just pouring water through it. Although the inch of space at the top of the pot generally can hold enough water to soak the root ball of the average-size plant, a large plant may need two or three waterings before the soil is thoroughly wet. If the water runs right through the soil and out the drainage hole, you can be sure the plant has been allowed to get so dry that it has shrunk in its pot and that you are watering the peat moss or sphagnum moss, instead of the root ball. Should this occur, the best solution is to repot the plant. When watering, be sure to put the water in the pot and not on the foliage.

Sometimes rapid growth is not desirable, especially when a foliage plant has reached the right size to fill its particular decorative purpose in the planter. Then you want the plant to grow slowly and maintain generally attractive proportions. Except where abundant light is available, rapid growth in certain plants results in soft, spindly and unattractive proportions.

Many of the foliage plants described in Chapter 4 can

be "trained" to maintain a slow rate of growth so they will remain attractive. This "training" involves keeping the soil moderately dry by using a system of alternate watering. One time the water is applied to the soil in the pots (enough so that the pot overflows slightly), and the next time the water is added to the peat moss or sphagnum moss surrounding the pots. By this method of culture, the soil can be kept moderately, but safely, dry for relatively long periods. This method of watering a planter is effective for the slow, healthy and attractive growth of foliage plants indoors, especially when they are in full shade. New plants may require a few days to adjust to dry culture. During this time they may require more frequent watering than "trained" plants. Do not, however, allow the plant, old or new, to wilt.

Do whatever watering is required in dull weather as early in the day as possible. No plant should be given frigid water directly from a tap. The natural source is temperate rain water. You can approximate this by letting the water stand in a pitcher until it is at room temperature.

While surface watering, properly done, is adequate, an occasional dunking, when feasible, will benefit the plants. To do this remove the plants from the planter and submerge the pots in a pail or tub of water to within 1" or 2" of their rims. Leave the pots in the water until the top of the soil is moist. Some planter gardeners give their plants a shower-and-soak all in one operation. To do this, place the plants in the bathtub, close the drain and turn the shower on gently at about room temperature. Spray the plants thoroughly (the undersides of the leaves, too), turn off the shower and continue filling the tub from the tap until the pots are nearly submerged. After an hour or so, drain the water from the tub and let the plants sit in this humid, shady spot until their leaves are completely dry before putting them back in the sun. The showering action leaves the foliage fresh, healthy and glossy, provides some temporary humidity and helps control insects; the soaking or dunking gets water to the entire root system. Those who follow this procedure regularly (every six to eight weeks), claim that their plants thrive better and require much less daily care and attention.

PLANT FOOD

The basic method of feeding is to mix the plant foods in the soil used in potting-up. These soil mixtures vary with the needs of the plants (see Chapter 8) and will generally be sufficient until the pot is filled with healthy roots. But as soon as this happens, the plant will need extra nourishment. Water is the means by which food in the soil is made available to plant roots, but it is not necessary to feed a plant each time you water it. Your planter's feeding schedule will depend on the size of the container, the type of plants and their stage of growth. Feed the plant more during the growing season, when new leaves and blossoms are being produced, than during its resting period. But, remember that a little plant food goes a long way—too much will not help and may burn the roots.

You can get water-soluble plant food from your local hardware or garden-supply dealer in two forms: dry (tablets, powder or granules) and liquid. Both forms give good results and it is wise to experiment with both to see which gives you best results. However, regardless of the type you use, measure carefully and follow the instructions on the container.

Water immediately after applying dry food to the soil to prevent burning. When using liquid food, use enough of the water solution to wet all of the soil. Generally, older plants benefit from a light feeding every month or so, while new plants or recently repotted ones usually need no extra food for the first six months. Since brands vary in strength, use the plant food as often as recommended by the manufacturer. Never use a solution stronger than recommended on the label, as it may injure the roots. A weak solution applied at frequent intervals is far better than a strong solution used only occasionally.

In general, foliage plants grown indoors under electric lighting require very little plant food. They should not be given more than about one-third as much as is recommended for the same plant grown in natural light.

CLEANING PLANTS

It is important to keep your plants clean so they will grow better and look better. Your plants collect just as much dust per square inch as your furniture. And dust on the top of leaves prevents light from getting through them for food-making. In general, a bulb syringe or house-plant sprayer filled with warm water will do the job, and the plant will always look fresher as a result. Do the syringing when the sun is not shining on the plants. You can avoid getting the soil wet by putting a paper collar around the rim of the pot. This syringing should be done once a week.

Smooth-leaved plants, such as rubber plant, philodendron or fiddle-leaf plant, require a more careful cleaning procedure. At least once a month, wipe the upper sides of the leaves with a soft damp cloth. Be sure to support each leaf from the bottom with your free hand. Use a mild detergent, or skimmed milk if the leaves are watermarked, and then clean with clear water. Never use oil on the leaves. If you do not get glossy foliage with the ordinary cleaning procedure, leaf conditioner (available from your local garden-supply dealer), can be applied according to the manufacturer's instructions.

Hairy-leaved plants can be washed with a warm spray, or brushed clean. A pipe cleaner, soft brush or surplus leaf makes a good cleaning tool. Brush gently toward the edges and tips of leaves.

Because of too-high room temperatures or lack of water, the leaves of some plants may turn brown at the tips and around the edges. There is no reason why these brown spots should remain to disfigure your plants. Simply cut away the dead leaf tissue with your scissors. If possible, shape the cut leaf to look like the undamaged leaves.

Many lush, large-leafed plants are so delicate that when moving them in the planter or syringing their foliage, you may break the ribs of the leaves. To mend the broken leaf, take a short length of thin, dark green silk thread, make a loop of it and encircle the leaf, holding the leaf in a natural position. In many cases, if the break is not too severe, the rib and surrounding leaf area will heal in time and you can remove the thread.

Completely dead leaves and stems, of course, should be removed. A small pair of scissors is good for this task. Never rip the dead parts off the plant with your fingers. Often the dead parts are still anchored to the plant, and you are likely to damage the living tissue.

DISEASES AND INSECTS

If your plants are cleaned regularly, you will have little trouble with insects, and probably no disease. Most insects breed in the oily dust of a warm room and spread from one plant to the next, until the entire planter becomes thoroughly infested. Inspect your plants at regular intervals for any signs of scale insects, mealybugs, spider mites (often called red spiders), plant lice and, in a few cases, worms at the roots. Actually, many planter gardeners give their plants a general pest-control treatment every month or so as a routine practice. This prevents small insects and less obvious diseases from getting a foothold unobserved.

When one plant seems badly affected by disease or insects, remove it from your planter and keep it quarantined until regular sprayings have brought it back to full health. Watch the rest of your plants for the first sign of infection. It is important when adding a new plant to your collection to be sure that the plant is healthy and will not bring insects into the planter. It is a good idea to isolate new plants until you are certain they are healthy. Most planter gardeners do not discover infected plants until it is too late to save them. You have to be suspicious and nosey. Regularly inspect all parts of the plant—leaves (particularly the undersides), stems and crowns—and if you find anything that looks suspicious, remove the plant from the container and treat it immediately.

If you use a sprayer to help control disease and insects —and you will have to on really large plants—be sure to cover all parts of the plant with the spray. One of the new aerosol sprayers will simplify your job, but make sure you get the right aerosol for your plants and their infection. When spraying, hold the sprayer at least a foot away from the plants. A cardboard shield will help you to make sure the spray gets only on the plants and *not* on the surrounding surfaces.

A description of the most common insects and diseases that affect plants in planters is given in the following paragraphs, together with suggestions for curing infected plants.

Scale insects have soft bodies and usually live under hard scales that may be round, oval or shaped somewhat like oyster or tortoise shells. Palms, citrus fruits, crotons, ivy, oleander and rubber plants are among those most frequently attacked by scale insects. The insects are difficult to detach from the plants. The soap-and-water treatment used for cleansing foliage is reasonably effective in destroying the insects. Another good cleansing solution can be made by dissolving 2 tablespoons of soap flakes (or 1 ounce of cake soap) in a gallon of water and then adding 1½ teaspoons of nicotine sulfate. This solution can be sprayed on the plants but is really more effective when applied by hand. A Malathion spray is also very good to use against scale insects.

Mealybugs, which look like little downy white tufts, are usually found along the veins on the underside of the leaves, in the leaf axils, or on the stems. They often form large masses which are difficult to get off the plant. To effectively eliminate mealybugs, use the soapsuds bath or the nicotine-sulfate-and-soap solution recommended for scale insects. After applying the cleansing solution, you will have to remove all the remaining insects by hand; a wisp of cotton fastened to a toothpick will be found helpful for this. A close search should be made each day until all the insects have disappeared. When it is practicable, the plants may be held under a faucet, or some other forceful stream of water, to wash off the insects. Treatment must be repeated frequently to keep mealybugs under control. A Malathion spray is also good to use against mealybugs.

Spider mites, or *red spiders* are little red or greenish mites that are difficult to see with the naked eye. They sometimes breed in large numbers and collect in tiny webs that they spin in the angles of the leaves where the petiole or leafstalk is attached to the stem of the plant. You can check the spread of spider mites with the soapsuds bath mentioned before or by frequent syringing of the plant with clear water. You can kill off the insects by spraying with contact insecticides, such as sprays containing Malathion, Aramite, derris extract or a derris root powder and soap solution. These insecticides should be used according to the directions on the label of the container. Dusting the plants with very fine sulfur (dusting sulfur), or with sulfur dust mixed with another insecticide is also of value.

Plant lice (aphids) are small, soft-bodied, sucking insects, which are green, brown or black in color. They usually collect on the underside of a leaf, causing the leaf to curl up and form a rooflike protection for the insect. These lice also collect on young stems. The soapsuds bath, a nicotine-sulfate-and-soap spray, DDT and Malathion, pyrethrum or derris sprays are all effective agents for controlling plant lice.

White flies cause leaves to turn yellow and die. They also excrete a honeydew on which a sooty fungus grows which blackens the plants. The young flies are light green in color and scalelike in appearance. The adults are very tiny, no larger than a pinhead, and are covered with a white powdery substance from which they derive their name. You can control white flies by spraying the infected plants two or three times a week with a nicotine-sulfate-and-soap solution or with the Malathion or derris sprays recommended for red spiders.

Tiny maggots or *worms* often found in the soil can

injure the roots of the plants. They are white harmless-looking creatures, very different from earthworms. The maggots eventually emerge into the air as small flies, called fungus gnats. An effective remedy is to drench the soil with a corrosive sublimate solution prepared by dissolving a 7½-grain tablet of bichloride of mercury in 1 pint of water. This solution is very poisonous and needs to be carefully handled. It should be prepared only in a glass or wooden container, as it corrodes metal. The tablets should be purchased only in quantities sufficient for immediate use, so that they will not have to be stored and thus be accessible to children or careless adults.

Thrips are slender, tiny black or yellow insects that are pointed at both ends and have almost invisible wings. They cause leaves to appear silvery and streaked, and then to turn brown and wilt. These quick-moving insects can be eliminated by spraying with Malathion, DDT or Lindane.

Snails and *slugs* (the latter are short, legless, shell-less creatures) live on leaves, around pot rims and in corners of planter boxes—in other words, any place that is dark and moist. They feed at night and hide during the daylight hours. Snails and slugs leave slimy tracks all over the foliage and eat ragged holes in the leaves. To get rid of them, pick off the snails and slugs (young children particularly enjoy doing this, but they can seldom resist starting a collection), or dust the plants with wood ashes. Dusting dries out their slimy bodies, and the exertion of moving about literally tires them to death.

In the absence of insects, leaves that develop white,

gray, yellow or brown spots are most likely affected by
mold, mildew, fungi, bacteria or viruses. But this seldom
occurs if the plants are given care and can usually be controlled by picking off the damaged leaves or cutting out
the infected parts. A dusting with powdered sulfur occasionally will also help. Burn any really badly affected
plants as they will not be worth saving.

Some plants, such as rubber plants and screw pines
(pandanus), are occasionally infected with fungus leaf
spots. When this occurs the damaged leaves should be
removed and destroyed, together with all plant debris in
or around the planter. Stop syringing the plant until the
fungus infection has been eliminated. The appearance of
fungus leaf spot on the rubber plant is sometimes the
result of the shock the plant experiences from a sudden
change in temperature. As fungus attacks on house plants
are almost always secondary infections, maintaining the
plant in vigorous health by providing favorable cultural
conditions is usually an adequate safeguard against them.
Black spots in the center of philodendron leaves generally
mean your plant is getting too much water.

General defoliation suggests gas poisoning, although it
may also be due to a sudden change in temperature, shock
from transplanting when the plants are in vigorous growth,
or a drastic change from strong sunlight to a dark place.
If after the leaves have dropped, the shoots remain
dwarfed, branch repeatedly, and put out small leaves, gas
injury or poisoning is further indicated. (Check the pilot
light on the kitchen range and other possible sources of

gas leakage.) Dying foliage from the base upward may also be caused by lack of light, improper watering or high temperature, in addition to gas injury.

Browning leaf tips suggest improper watering (overwatering or underwatering), exposure to drafts, cold air or insect attacks. With aspidistras, the leaf tips may turn brown because not enough water is reaching the ball of earth itself when the plant is watered or because the plant is exposed to full sunshine before it is hardened to this excessive heat. Browning and drying edges and spots on the foliage may also be caused by an accumulation of salts in the potting soil. Salts will collect in the soil when the water drains through too slowly. This can be corrected by repotting with the proper soil mixture and making sure that all the watering that you do has a flushing, leaching effect. In the case of palms, such browning may mean that there are worms on the roots or that the plant is not getting enough food.

Sometimes browning at the leaf tips is due to the fact that the foliage is touching a glass surface. This is quite common during really hot or cold weather when the planter is located in front of a glass wall or a large picture window. As stated previously in Chapter 3, solid glass areas can become very hot or very cold and often burn or freeze the soft growth that is located close to them. If large plants cannot be screened by blinds or draperies, they should be set back at least 3′ from glass areas. Smaller plants can be protected on very sunny days or cold nights by placing a piece of newspaper or cardboard or some other insulating material between the glass and the foliage.

Plant rot may develop anywhere along the stems of the plants, in the crowns and the leaves, at the soil surfaces, or in the roots. One of the symptoms of plant rot at the roots is lifeless, limp foliage—the plant looks as if it needs water although the soil is sufficiently wet. To overcome a minor case of plant rot, simply cut away and burn the diseased tissue. A dusting with powdered sulfur is good, too. Root rot can sometimes be overcome by drenching the soil with zineb. After this treatment, keep the plant fairly dry; avoid wetting the leaves until the growth is healthy again. If the plant is badly affected by rot or if rotting occurs at the base, it is best to discard it.

Yellowing foliage may be caused by excessive use of plant food, overwatering or poor light. The roots are usually injured. If one of these three conditions is definitely not the cause and the pots are full of roots (which can be corrected by repotting) plant food may be needed or the soil may be too alkaline. Such plants may as well be discarded unless they can be revived by applications of plant food.

Loss of normal color in the foliage suggests overwatering, lack of plant food or insect attacks, especially scale insects, mealybugs and spider mites. Spotted foliage suggests overwatering or burning from exposure to direct sunlight on foliage that is not accustomed to it. Dead areas on the edges of leaves are the result of injury to the roots by improper feeding or watering. Dead spots on the leaves are caused by excessive sunlight, dry soil, disease or insects. It is a good idea to rotate the position of the plants in your planter occasionally so that all the foliage will receive equal light.

PINCHING AND PRUNING

Many plants will become tall and ungainly-looking unless they are pinched to cause branching. Branching may be desirable to make a plant bushier and fuller, or to keep it shorter than it would otherwise be. Pinching consists of removing the very tip of the plant by pinching it off between your fingernails or cutting it with a knife. It is always much better to pinch a plant as soon as it reaches the desired height, rather than waiting until the plant has grown to the point where you will have to pinch off more than 4″ to 6″ of the shoot. The smaller the shoot that is removed, the less shock to the plant.

Pruning is a more severe operation than pinching. It involves cutting mature plant growth. It is usually done to promote shapeliness, to maintain size limits or to remove weak and crowded shoots. The time to prune, except for dead or hopelessly diseased growths, which should be removed as soon as they appear, varies according to the kind of plant. Use a sharp knife and make a slanting cut just a little above the stem node or joint. Be sure to make clean cuts.

While the aerial roots of philodendron and similar plants can be pruned as far back as the stem, it is generally best not to take them off entirely, for these roots serve a useful purpose even indoors. Since aerial roots help supply oxygen to the plant, they may aid in overcoming a poor drainage condition. Aerial roots hanging down or laying on the planter medium can be bent up and tucked down into the soil.

When plants get too large for a planter, they may be replaced with new plants of the proper size. Or you can propagate smaller plants from the old one. Most house plants can be easily propagated by the planter gardener. (See Chapter 9 for details.)

SUMMER CARE FOR HOUSE PLANTS

Small plants in stationary or portable planters may be used outdoors to decorate porches or terraces in the summertime. True, this has a good reconditioning effect on the plants, but since planters are actually pieces of furniture and make a definite decorative contribution to the interior of your home, you will probably not want to set all your plants outdoors. It is best to have separate planters for exterior use (see Chapter 3).

If you take individual plants out of the planter or put your entire portable unit outdoors, the plants should receive approximately the same amount of sunlight as they were accustomed to indoors. They may be placed in exterior-type planters or in garden beds. Setting pots in exterior planters or garden beds is discussed in detail in Chapter 7. But wherever the plants are placed outdoors, they should be protected against strong winds and grouped to facilitate watering and syringing. Do not remove the plants from their containers because in an open planter or garden bed they will develop such ranging root systems that autumn repotting will involve so severe a root pruning as to retard growth.

Plants set outdoors cannot be forgotten in summer. Because of their restricted root systems and general location, they require more frequent watering than the average summer rainfall supplies. Some pruning may be necessary to promote shapely growth. And, of course, you must continue to inspect the plants for signs of insects. Usually frequent hose syringing will deter these pests but sometimes the mealybugs or plant lice will require spraying with an insecticide.

Before returning the plants to the house, the outsides of all pots should be scrubbed clean with a brush and soap and water. The top soil should be removed down to the roots and replaced with the proper soil mixture to which bone meal has been added at the rate of 1 teaspoonful to each 4″ pot. You can eliminate a great deal of trouble and contribute to the future welfare of your plants by thoroughly cleaning them of any insect pests before they are brought into the house. To replace the plants in the planter, dig a hole in the moss and plunge the pot in until the rim remains slightly above the moss. Then pack the moss around the pot.

If a cold spell catches your plants outdoors and they freeze, take them in the house immediately before the sun

PLATE 19: The planter box at the left of this built-in desk adds interest to the design. (*Courtesy, Hardwood Plywood Institute; Designer, Paul Haberfeld.*)

PLATE 20: A corner planter creates an indoor garden in this porch.

PLATE 21: An under-the-window planter conceals an ugly radiator and adds a pleasant touch to this window.

PLATE 22: An effective arrangement of foliage plants in a picture-window planter bin.

has had a chance to thaw them out and place them in a lighted basement where the temperature is cold but not freezing. There they will have the opportunity to thaw out slowly and the chances are *fair* that they will survive.

SEVEN • Selecting and Arranging Plants in an Exterior Planter

Color . . . Variety . . . Quick effects . . . Easy care . . . For these reasons, we see more and more families putting outdoor flowers and even house plants into stationary and portable exterior planters. And these planters are ideal for today's small gardens which start at the house door or terrace.

SELECTING PLANTS FOR AN EXTERIOR PLANTER

Success with exterior planters is not difficult, although you may have to learn some new gardening rules. To get off to the right start, you must choose your plants carefully. Your first consideration must be the physical conditions under which the plants will grow. Will they be in full sun, partial sun or full shade? Is the location subject to the buffetings of prevailing winds, or is it sheltered, offering the proper encouragement to plant growth?

The foliage and flowering plants listed in Chapter 4 are suitable for use in exterior planters during the summer months. For the most part, foliage plants have been much more successful than flowering species. The same cultural conditions described in Chapter 4 must be followed when the plants are outdoors and care must be exercised to bring them in before the cold weather sets in. Some small shrubs and trees are suitable for year-round use in exterior planters.

In addition, annuals and perennials may be successfully used. In general, perennials offer a more subtle and spectacular range of color than annuals and, if carefully selected, may be arranged to produce blooms throughout the growing season. While most perennials prefer sunlight, there are several varieties that will do very well in shade, too. But, regardless of where they are located, all perennials require plenty of water and periodic feedings with plant food. Actually, some perennials will exhaust the nutrients in the planter soil during the course of one season. Since perennials are deep-rooted and increase in size each year, they must be divided every one to three years into smaller clumps. But, remember that in a planter (unlike a garden border or plot), the more plants that are crowded into the container, the more luxurious the bloom will be. (Like potted plants that are pot-bound, their energy goes into producing flowers instead of roots.) The soil should be reworked when the plants are broken up. Finally, you should not expect too much color from perennials in a planter during the first year. After the seeds are sown it generally takes from two to four years for perennials to develop their full capacity for bloom. You can reduce this waiting period by purchasing nursery-grown or pot-planted perennials.

Of the sun-loving perennials, some of the most successful for use in planters are: chrysanthemums, irises, poppies, English daisies, pinks, geraniums, perennial candytuft, pyrelbrum, *Sedum sieboldii, Arabis alpina*, dianthus, coreopsis and achillea. Tulips, hyacinths, amaryllis, daffodils, narcissuses and other spring-flowering bulbs are also suitable for sunny planters.

In planters located in full or partial shade, the following perennials may be used: aquilegia, begonias (many varieties), trailing or dwarf campanulas, Christmas rose (*Helleborus niger*), varieties of bleeding heart, *Francoa ramosa* and primroses. Indoor plants like fancy-leaved begonias, caladiums, patience plants, gloxinias and foliage plants like chlorophytum, dracaena and philodendron thrive in small shady planters, especially in kitchen window boxes. Chives, basil, burnet, hyssop, mint, parsley, pot marjoram, sage, tarragon and thyme are also worth trying. A kitchen window box filled with herbs has always been a favorite with cooks.

On the whole, annuals are the most satisfactory for use in planters because they come and go at fairly definite times, whereas perennials are likely to be irregular. Also, annuals, being temporary, can be planted thickly. They may be started in pots or flats indoors during the winter or the early spring and then set out in planters to give you early blossoming in the garden. The water, soil and plant-food requirements of annuals are moderate but most of them prefer sunshine. (When potted annuals or perennials are in bloom, you can move them to shaded planters. They do need sun to bloom but, once open, they will last longer in the shade.) Since annuals have shallow root systems, they are very suitable for shallow planters and window boxes.

Of the many flowering annuals, the most popular ones include: petunias, asters, marigolds, cynoglossums, calendulas, zinnias, delphiniums, nicotiana, portulacas, torenias, phlox, lobelias, ageratums, browallias, scabiosas, alyssums, dwarf dahlias, pansies, amethysts, cerastiums, nasturtiums, celosias and snapdragons. For further information on growing perennials and annuals, I would suggest reading such

books as *Perennials For Every Garden* by Helen Van Pelt
Wilson and *Annuals For Every Garden* by Dorothy
Jenkins.

Color in Exterior Planters

When using flowering house plants, shrubs, perennials
and annuals in exterior planters, some thought should be
given to the general color scheme. What is the color of
your house? Brick, for instance, will not be enhanced by
planters full of blue petunias, red geraniums or crimson
zinnias. Green and white, or pale yellow would be successful color choices for a brick house. A white house, on the
other hand, is a good background for all colors. And a
stone house will show the lighter and brighter hues to
good advantage. You should also consider nearby permanent plantings and flower beds. In other words, let your
imagination and taste have full sway in choosing colors
for your planter, so long as your selections do not clash
with the surrounding landscape. Remember that large,
concentrated splashes of color will give the greatest effect
if your planter is viewed from a distance.

Portable planters are the simplest way to produce quick
changes in color. With these containers, it is possible to
bring plants into bloom under the best soil conditions, set
them in place and achieve the same effect as flowering
beds. With two sets of containers, you can keep one set
on display while you are bringing the other set into bloom.

In addition to using planter boxes as spot or accent
decoration, one of their most popular exterior applications

is to use them in place of foundation planting around windows, especially when the windows extend to the floor. In such a location, some of the boxes may be planted with slow-growing, permanent evergreen shrubs such as small specimens of holly, myrtle, euonymus, yew and boxwood; while in alternate boxes, you may wish to rotate the seasonal color of spring bulbs and summer and fall annuals and perennials. Experimenters have found, too, that boxes need not always be placed on solid surfaces such as terraces, patios or walks. The planter-box system works equally well when the boxes are sunk into the ground like flower beds.

On large, exterior walls, you might try placing the boxes in steps or tiers to give a very attractive bank of color. If you use three tiers of boxes, for instance, you might plant them in the following manner: in the first tier use low plants such as pansies, petunias, portulacas, lobelias, pinks, nasturtiums, helianthemums, nierembergias and calendulas; in the next one use medium-sized annuals such as marigolds, zinnias and dwarf stock; and in the final row use background plants such as dwarf dahlias, snapdragons, cleomes, delphiniums, larkspurs and chrysanthemums. Bulbs and groundcovers are also excellent possibilities for tiered arrangements of planter boxes. You might, for example, try a combination of crocuses, galanthuses and chionodoxas or alyssums and aubrietias; or irises, amaryllis and lilies or linarias; or daffodils, narcissuses and tulips or candytuft and primulas.

You can also choose plants for stationary exterior

planters in such a way that there will be continuous bloom and foliage throughout the year. By planning ahead and using potted plants, you can make your planters brilliant spots of beauty almost the year round instead of just at the height of the summer season. It might, for example, be done as follows: open the spring with a spread of hyacinths followed by tulips. Then could come geraniums or begonias, followed by summer-blooming annuals such as petunias, marigolds, zinnias and calendulas. In the fall, you could use chrysanthemums and complete the year with evergreen plants such as English ivy, small specimens of boxwood, Japanese holly, arborvitae and dwarf yew that can withstand frost. For help in the planning of such arrangements, I would suggest writing to the Extension Service, Cornell University, Ithaca, New York for their bulletin #21, "Sequences of Blooms of Perennials, Biennials and Bulbs."

Plant Size

When selecting plants for stationary exterior planters, keep in mind the three main types of growth: plants that grow tall enough to make a good background, plants that grow 8" to 18" tall and will form the center of interest in the planter, and plants that will trail down over edges of the container. For example, you may wish to use evergreens as a background, while using medium-sized plants such as geraniums, begonias (*B. semperflorens*) and coleuses as central decoration. (Any of these plants that start to grow too tall may be pinched back.) Low-growing plants for filler in the front of the planter could be sweet alyssum, ageratum, verbena, browallia, lobelia and portulaca; the trailers could be ivy, *Vinca major,* trailing nasturtiums or balcony petunias. But, regardless of the plants you decide to use, be sure to consider and take advantage of all three heights when making arrangements for large planters.

As I have already suggested, vines are very suitable to use in stationary exterior planters. (You will seldom find them used in portable types.) When vines are trained on a sturdy trellis attached to the planter, they will provide an attractive background, while other species are well suited for growing as hanging trailers over the edge of planters and window boxes. While almost any species of vine will grow in a planter, the slow-growing varieties, such as the ivies and those that do not put out large root systems, will keep their appearance best. Fast-growing types with hawserlike stems usually outgrow the planter too rapidly.

Most shrubs and many trees will grow successfully in large stationary and portable units. Actually, some species seem to thrive better in the restricted root area offered by such containers. But they must be plants of intrinsic beauty with textures and forms that will hold interest through the seasons. Slow-growing small or medium-sized shrubs or small trees that mature slowly and do not change quickly in relation to their architectural setting and to other plants around them are preferable, too. Of course, some plants can spend their youthful years in a planter and, when their root systems have increased, can be transplanted into your landscape plan.

When selecting trees and shrubs for planter use, you should also consider color, plant structure, leaf texture, and whether a single specimen or a mass of plants is called for to produce the desired mood or effect. For example, if a soft, rather finely textured effect is desired, varying sizes of cutleaf European white birch, azaleas, Japanese pieris, and the common periwinkle might be your choices. For a bold, more dramatic mass effect, leucothoë, flowering dogwood and rosebay rhododendron, which are relatively coarse-textured and strong in character, might be selected. This last arrangement would also provide year-round interest in the planter. For instance, dogwood has either pink or white flowers in the spring, red berries and leaves in the fall, and artistic-looking bare branches in the winter.

Other deciduous trees and shrubs, like dogwood, that can provide year-round seasonal interest for your planter are blueberry (*Vaccinium corymbosum*), viburnum (*Viburnum sieboldi*), symplocos (*Symplocos paniculata*), photinia and firethorn (*Pyracantha coccinea lalandi*). Among the evergreen there are mountain laurel (*Kalmia latifolia*), hollies, Pfitzer junipers, cotoneasters, euonymus, yews and dwarf Japanese andromedas (*Pieris japonica compacta*). Even some dwarf varieties of flowering fruit trees will do well in planters; I have known of some trees that have spent their entire productive lives in planter units or boxes.

Tall grasses can be as interesting and pleasing as shrubs and trees in your planter. Of the many suitable varieties of grasses, the most impressive and popular is Chinese silver grass or eulalia (*Miscanthus sinesis variegatus*). This plant has a fairly bushy base that sends up many long, graceful beige-colored stems, terminating in a feathery plume of golden yellow. The stems and plumes last through most of the winter, offering an effect rarely seen in the ordinary garden. Other good grasses for planter use include blue lily turf (*Liriope muscari*) and horsetail grass (*Equisetum hyemale*).

Vegetable Gardens

While it may sound ridiculous, I have seen vegetables grown very successfully in both stationary and portable planters. Some vegetables naturally respond to planter applications. Many are so good-looking in their own right that you can consider them as ornamental plants and forget they are called vegetables. Leafy, frilly vegetables and herbs, such as parsley, chervil and lettuce, are good examples. If you plant a row of begonias, lobelias or dwarf ageratums in front of the vegetables, you need not concern yourself about the bare spots that will appear as you harvest the leafy vegetables.

Rhubarb chard, with its large red leaves, is another vegetable that has long been looked upon as ornamental, both in the garden and in flower arrangements. The first time I saw chard in a planter it was set among tall, white sweet William and dwarf phlox, and made a most attractive planter. Incidentally, rhubarb itself, with its large, glossy, deeply crinked green leaves on red stems can be used to produce the same effect as half-grown *Fatsia japonica* and acanthus. Actually, rhubarb, and its gray counterpart, artichoke, make handsome plants even for your interior planters.

PLANTING AN EXTERIOR PLANTER

To maintain a constant display of color in your exterior planter, the plants can be grown in pots (indoors or out), and simply transferred to the planter by sinking the containers in the soil, peat moss or vermiculite just before the plants reach full bloom. If you do not want to grow annuals or perennials in pots, you can dig them from your garden just as buds appear and move them to the planter. Carefully lift each plant, making sure there is a good-sized ball of soil around the roots. It is important that you take care to disturb the roots as little as possible. Place the plants in the planter to the same depth they grew at in the garden soil, and space them close together. Water them thoroughly after planting. Annual seeds may be sown directly in the open soil of a planter, and then treated in the same manner as if they were being cultivated in flats. Of course, this method will not give you the variety of bloom possible with potted plants since the planter is limited to one crop.

As you can see, plants may be grown either in the open soil in the planter or in pots. The latter arrangement, as in the case of interior planters, has many advantages and should be used whenever possible. The pots or containers

are placed in soil, peat moss or vermiculite and the rims
are set level with or slightly above the embedding material.
Peat moss or vermiculite is ideal for small planters, while
soil is best to use in the larger units or the bottomless
types that rest directly on the ground.

Various soil mixtures suitable for exterior planters are
discussed in Chapter 8, and general cultural characteristics
of flowering and foliage plants have been covered in
Chapter 4. Plant the plants in containers as described in
Chapter 8. Be sure to keep the soil at least an inch below
the rim of the container, so that a single watering is sufficient to wet the soil down to the bottom of the pot. Any
good porous soil may be used as a base and filler for pots.

If plants are to be grown in the open soil in a planter,
use the standard soil mixture and to each bushel of the
mixture add 1 pint of plant food (enough to fill a 4″
flowerpot). Fill the planter with soil up to a couple of
inches from the top. Every three or four weeks add plant
food to the soil according to the directions given on the
package. Occasionally loosen the soil with a small fork
or hand cultivator, but do not disturb the roots. Some
planter gardeners put an inch or so of peat-moss mulch
over the entire surface of the soil. They claim that this will
keep the soil moist for longer periods of time and will dis-
courage the growth of weeds in the planter.

Regardless of the type of exterior planter you have or
whether you set your plants in open soil or in pots, be sure
to cover the bottom of the planter with a few inches of
crushed rock or gravel. And as an extra precaution against

improper drainage, place a layer of peat moss, sphagnum moss or excelsior over the gravel before filling the planter with soil or filler. The excess moisture collected in the gravel is allowed to escape through the wall. This results in what frequently is described as a "moist but well-drained growing condition." Lines of open-joint agricultural tile may be installed in the drainage base to direct water to the wall, but this is seldom necessary. Do not forget to bridge the drainage holes in window planter boxes to prevent the soil from washing out as the plants are watered by placing a curved piece of broken flowerpot or pottery over each hole.

CARING FOR PLANTS IN AN EXTERIOR PLANTER

Nothing could be gayer and do more to beautify your home than exterior planters filled with well-chosen, well-tended and healthy plants; but nothing is more forlorn and depressing-looking than gangling, half-dead flowers or dried-up foliage in planters. Planters can be plant coffins and often they look like it, too.

An exterior planter requires more watering than the interior type, since the sun and the hot air will cause the moisture to evaporate more quickly outdoors. Rain water may not penetrate to the soil because of the position of the planter or the foliage of the plants in it. Plants set in open soil often require daily watering, while those in pots, especially when set in peat moss, will not need to be watered so frequently. But be sure moisture gets below the surface of the soil so it will never dry out completely. Also be careful to keep the planter free of weeds.

In cold weather, planter plants are more likely to freeze than their cousins growing in garden beds. Stationary units should be well mulched and covered with straw in addition to the standard winter protection you give your other garden plants. The portable types may be moved to a protected area or covered with plastic film, burlap or some other lightweight material.

The insect and disease control for house plants discussed in Chapter 6 should also be applied to the plants that are set outdoors in planters. For information on the care of annuals and perennials, I would suggest that you read one of the previously mentioned books on the subject. Earthworms can sometimes cause trouble for the planter gardener. If earthworms invade your planter, you can chase them out by soaking the soil with a limewater solution made of 8 teaspoons of slaked lime to 1 gallon of water. Be sure to watch the plants carefully to see if they can take the limewater solution without harm.

When plants are placed in open soil, especially trees and shrubs, the pH value (acidity or alkalinity of the soil) should be checked. This may be done easily with a soil-testing kit available at your garden center. (Instructions are furnished with the kit.) Faulty soil may be corrected with the proper chemicals. For further information on soil testing, I would suggest that you write for a free copy of "Soil Testing—A Practical System of Soil Fertility Diagnosis" by Spurway and Lawton, Technical Bulletin 132, Michigan State College Agricultural Experiment Station, East Lansing, Michigan.

The art of pinching (discussed in Chapter 6) is one practice you must follow if you want your flowering plants to look their best. Nipping back the tips of chrysanthemums, dianthus, nasturtiums, pansies, marigolds, dahlias, daisies and other flowering plants causes them to throw out more stems and buds and encourages a tidy, compact, bushy system of growth. To keep your planter neat, tie the plants to short stakes so they will stand upright. Stain the stakes green to blend inconspicuously with the foliage. Be sure to pick off faded blossoms, seed pods or yellowing leaves as soon as they appear. This will allow the plants to bloom for a longer period of time and will prevent the planter from getting a "ragged" look. After all, your planter is on view constantly and your plants should always look in tip-top condition.

EIGHT • Potting and Repotting

The purpose of soil in the planter is to provide nutrients and to hold moisture. To do this job well, the soil will have to be renewed occasionally. If you enrich the soil from time to time, many plants will be able to live for years in the same mixture. Usually small-sized containers and pots will have exhausted their nutrients after a year or so. Of course, you can add nutrients, but the soil itself should be renewed after a period of time. Generally, however, the plant will indicate to you when the soil is no longer doing its job—that is, watch the plant rather than the calendar.

SOIL MIXTURES

When you prepare soil for planters, whether the plants are going to be planted in pots or in open soil, remember that the physical state of the soil is even more important than its chemical composition. In other words, the primary requirement for any planter soil is adequate drainage.

Plants need well-drained soil in varying degrees of porosity; most plants require fairly rapid draining while others can take slower draining; but no plants suitable for planters will grow in water-logged soil. Their roots require plenty of air. In order to insure a constant supply of air, the soil must encourage good drainage and so should consist of fairly coarse particles. Soil that is perfectly satisfactory for outdoor gardening may be quite unsuitable for planter use. Plants growing in containers exist under artificial conditions. Their soil is usually more firmly packed than garden soil and is watered more often so that planter soil quickly becomes drained of nutrients and filled with roots. Because of this planter soil should be specially mixed.

In general, then, your planter plants will grow better and require less care if the soil you use is combined with ingredients that will provide better drainage, hold additional moisture and increase fertility. If you start with the best possible garden soil, you can transform it into an excellent planter mixture by adding a few ingredients.

The first of these ingredients is a coarse grade of sand, such as that used by builders. Sand is needed to insure good drainage and improve aeration. Adequate substitutes are finely crushed brick, flowerpots and crocks, coarse cinders or gravel. Never use a soft, silky white sand since it will pack even more closely than soil.

After the sand you will need to add leaf mold, humus or peat moss to provide nutrients and to hold moisture. Leaf mold is the name given the half-decayed leaves that you find lying under the freshly fallen leaves in autumn. Beech and oak leaves are best, but foliage from any non-evergreen tree will do. Rub the leaves together until they reach a flaky consistency. Leaf mold has excellent texture and is also a good plant food. Humus lies under leaf mold and is a fine, black, completely disintegrated substance that is readily available by the package. It makes excellent plant food. Peat moss is a sterile mixture of partially decayed organic matter which comes commercially prepared. It has good texture but little food value. Of these three materials, leaf mold is the most desirable because it provides both texture and food. However, because leaf mold does not come commercially prepared, it is harder to work with. Therefore, an equal mixture of humus and peat moss is better for the planter gardener to use.

To enrich your soil mixture still further, use a combination of bone meal and well-rotted cow manure or sheep manure. The bone meal can be added at the rate of 1 teaspoon to each 4″ pot (1 pint of soil). For larger amounts of soil, the amount should be increased proportionately. An all-purpose commercial fertilizer may be substituted for the bone meal.

In general, the more common house plants for planter use can be placed in one of the following four soil mixture groups:

For 90 Per Cent of All Plants (Average Soil Mixture)

2 parts good garden soil
1 part leaf mold, humus or peat moss
1 part coarse sand
½ part manure and bone meal

For Humus-Loving Plants

Same as above, but quadruple the amount of leaf mold, humus or peat moss recommended and increase the manure by 50 per cent. Throw in 1 quart of finely broken charcoal to each bushel if you have it. (If you have a wood-burning fireplace, it is worth while to save small amounts of charcoal to "sweeten" the soil mixture.)

For Acid-Soil Plants

2 parts good garden soil
2 parts coarse sand
2 parts peat moss
1 part leaf mold
⅓ part manure

For Plants Demanding Extra-Good Drainage

2 parts good garden soil
2 parts coarse sand

2 parts leaf mold

2 parts finely crushed bricks or crocks

In each of these mixtures, be sure that all the ingredients are thoroughly mixed. For best results, soak leaf mold, humus or peat moss in water overnight, and then squeeze out all excess water just before mixing the soil. To achieve the proper blending of ingredients in your mixture, turn the pile of soil with your hands until it is all one color and the sand is no more distinct than the soil or leaf mold.

If you wish to eliminate the work involved in preparing good planting mixtures, ready-mixed potting soils similar to the ones already described are available from most florists or garden centers. Whether you make your own soil mixture or buy special potting soil, always repot or replant with a damp mixture, never with dry soil. A good test for dampness is the same as the standard one for all soil texture: take a handful of soil and squeeze hard. If any water comes out, the soil is too wet; if the soil falls apart quickly when your hand is opened, it is too dry; but if the soil retains its shape or merely cracks slightly, it is proper dampness. For convenience, store prepared soil in plastic bags to keep it moist.

The suggested "recipes" for soil mixtures given previously are arbitrary. Do not take them too literally. Vary the ingredients to suit special circumstances and experiment with your own combinations when the opportunity presents itself. Beware, however, of the common error of sifting your materials too much and getting a mixture so fine that it packs down when the soil is watered and prevents air from getting to the roots.

REPOTTING AND REPLANTING

With planter plants, it is far more difficult to learn *when* to pot than it is to learn *how* to pot. Generally, the best time to transfer potted plants is at the close of the resting season, usually in late winter or early spring. Young plants which are still actively growing should be transferred when the pots become so filled with roots that growth is likely to be impeded. For most plants, however, repotting need not be an annual operation. Moving a plant to a larger pot is not a panacea for all the ills that beset plants in planters. If a plant fails to thrive because of unsuitable soil, overwatering or poor drainage, transferring it to a larger pot will only accentuate the trouble.

In general, plants require repotting when the pot is crowded with roots and the available plant food nutrients in the soil are exhausted. But in the case of planter plants, it is worthwhile first to consider whether the plant cannot be kept healthy by an operation known as "top dressing." This simply means removing the loose soil on the surface and replacing it with a mixture of half good-garden-soil and half rotted-cow-manure, with bone meal added at the rate of 1 teaspoon to a 4" pot (1 pint of soil). Before the top dressing is applied, remove the plant from its pot and, if the drainage has become clogged, correct the trouble before returning the plant to the pot. Subsequent supplementary feedings with liquid nutrients (fertilizers dis-

PLATE 23: Metal stands are ideal for displaying single potted house-plants.

PLATE 24: Trailing begonia leaves create a graceful arrangement in hanging planter.

PLATE 25: An exterior planter used as an integral part of the architectural facade adds richness to this terrace.

PLATE 26: Effective use of portable and hanging planters on several levels to decorate an outdoor patio.

PLATE 27: A Spanish wrought-iron wall bracket with begonias creates an interesting decorative note.

solved in water) usually are desirable for pot-bound plants. If, however, the pot is so full of roots that no soil can be removed from the surface, then you can be reasonably sure that a shift to a larger pot is in order.

The first step in repotting is to provide clean pots of suitable sizes. If new pots are used, it is best to soak them for an hour or so in water, so that when you do your re-potting and water the new plant, the water will go to the plant and not be soaked up by the new pot.

When re-using old pots, make sure that they are very clean, otherwise you may be troubled by mold and fungus. To do a complete job, place the pots in a bucket or tub of hot soapy water to which a little household bleach has been added. Scrub them thoroughly with a stiff brush and rinse them several times in clear water. After the pots have dried for 48 hours (this will allow the bleach to evaporate) they may be treated in the same manner as new ones.

The pot into which the plant is to be transferred should not be much larger than the old one. Usually 1″ to 1½″ of clearance between the ball of earth and the side of the pot is adequate. If you use too large a pot, the soil will remain too wet because you get less thorough aeration. Adequate drainage is secured by covering the hole in the bottom of the pot with a piece of broken flowerpot, concave side down; this in turn is covered with a layer (½″ to 1″ deep) of flowerpot chips. On top of this, a ¼″ to ⅜″ layer of coarse organic material, such as flaky leaf mold, is placed. The coarse material will prevent fine soil from sifting through and clogging the drainage.

Plants that are to be repotted should be watered well a few hours beforehand. If transplanted when dry they are bound to suffer more than if their tissues are charged with moisture. Do not, however, soak them immediately before repotting. If you do, the soil will be so wet that you are bound to puddle it in the potting procedure. Allow the soil to drain for a short period before attempting to transplant.

To remove the plant from the pot, turn the pot upside down and tap the rim firmly against the edge of a table or potting bench. Do not hold the pot with one hand while you yank at the plant with the other. As you tap the old pot, cover its mouth with your hand to catch the ball of soil when it slides out. If the specimen is too large to be handled in this manner, take hold of the plant at the base of the stem, lift the pot slightly above the ground and tap the rim with a piece of wood or a wooden mallet. Carefully examine the ball and remove any loose surface soil along with the old drainage material if it is not too firmly held in place by the crowded roots.

Now you are ready for the actual potting process. Place the plant in the center of the new pot. You may add a little soil over the drainage material, if necessary, to bring the ball of earth to the proper height in the new pot. Actually, it is very important to set the plant in place so it is neither too low nor too high in the pot. If it is placed too far down, it will not have sufficient room for proper root development and if it is located too high, its roots will not be able to fill in the pot rapidly enough to prevent soil from souring. A good rule to follow is to place the old ball of earth approximately an inch below the rim of the new pot.

After setting the plant at the proper level, fill in around the roots with the correct soil mixture. Settle the soil in the pot by jarring it on the top of the potting bench or table. It is desirable that the new earth should be packed to the same density as that in the old pot. You can pack the new soil with a potting stick or a piece of wood lath until it is evenly firm throughout the entire pot. When the soil is uniformly packed, finish off by pressing down the surface soil and leveling it with the tips of your fingers; then give the pot a slight jar on the bench or table to loosen the surface soil. Never fill a pot up to the top. Leave a space about one-half of the depth of the rim to provide room for convenient watering.

When the potting task is completed, thoroughly water the soil. If the water passes through rapidly, tamp the soil; if the water remains on top, the soil needs loosening. Do not water again until the soil shows signs of becoming dry. Great care should be exercised to avoid overwatering the plant before new roots have had a chance to establish themselves.

To keep the topsoil in the pot cultivated, use an old kitchen fork. Occasionally, when the soil is dry, rake it to a depth of about half an inch. Do not go any deeper, for you may injure the roots.

Plants in Metal Containers

As stated in Chapter 2, metal (not copper) containers are sometimes substituted for clay pots in exterior planter arrangements and for larger plants. When it is necessary to repot a plant in a metal container, it generally means that the container must be cut away from the plant. To make certain that the ball of earth will not break during the cutting process, water the plant thoroughly. If the plant cannot be removed from the container in the same way as from a pot, split the container open by using a metal cutting device. After cutting the metal, the two edges of the container may be spread apart and the entire ball of soil lifted out.

To replant, set the plant gently into the new container on a cushion of loam over a layer of pebbles. The top of the root ball should be placed 1″ or 2″ below the top of the container. Fill in the remaining space around the plant with soil, tamping it down as you go along, and water thoroughly.

Replanting a Planter

When plants are set in open soil in a planter, the soil may need to be replaced. When this is necessary, soak the soil with water a few hours before digging the plants out of the planter. Take a good-sized ball of earth with each plant and use a fork for digging rather than a trowel to preserve as many roots as possible. After you have removed the plants, take out all the old soil from the planter and replace with a new mixture. The plants then can be put back into the soil in the same manner as described in Chapter 7. But, no matter how careful you are, each plant will lose some of its roots. Therefore, you will need to cut back the tops of the plants to get a fairer balance between the root system and the amount of stems and leaves it must support. Ordinarily, anywhere from one-third to one-half of the top growth may be pruned to advantage.

NINE • Propagating New Plants

New plants are needed from time to time for your planters. Some may not grow well or simply just not be attractive-looking, while others will grow too big to be of value. New plants, of course, may be purchased from your local florist or nurseryman or from one of the other sources for planter equipment given in the Appendix. Or, you may want to propagate new plants from your old ones.

In the late spring or early summer is usually a good time to reshape or propagate interior planter plants. After spending the winter indoors, the plants may be leggy and in need of pinching and cutting back (see Chapter 6 for details). You can generally start new plants with the pieces you have removed. Actually, there are four common methods by which you can propagate house plants: stem cuttings, leaf cuttings, divisions, and layering (either by ground or air).

STEM CUTTINGS

A large variety of plants can easily be propagated by stem cuttings. A representative sampling of varieties would include: arrowhead vines (*Syngonium podophyllum* and *S. albolineatum*), *Pilea microphylla*, *Helxine Soleirolii*, begonias, bougainvillaea, *Calathea Vandenheckei*, Chinese evergreen and holly, Coleus, *Cissus discolor*, dracaenas, *Peristrophe augustifolia aureo-variegata*, dieffenbachia, evergreen grape, *Fatsia japonica*, Pothos, *Maranta bicolor* and *M. tricolor*, geraniums, gold-dust plant, grape ivy, *Senecio mikanio ides*, kangaroo vine, wandering Jew, most ivies and many species of philodendron.

To make a stem cutting or "slip," select a piece of half-mature growth along the stem about 2" to 3" long, with two or three sets of leaves attached (see Fig. 22). Then, with a sharp knife, cut the stem from the parent plant just below a leaf node (one of the knots or sections into which a stem divides itself). Remove the foliage from the lowest

Fig. 22: Method of making a stem cutting.

knot, because it is from this node that the new roots will grow. After you have taken several cuttings, they may be placed in a rooting medium—such as sand, sand and peat moss, vermiculite or water. Many planter gardeners have found that dipping the cut end of the slip into hormone powder before it is placed in the rooting medium will hasten rooting.

Typical of the plants which will root in water alone are wandering Jew, Chinese evergreen, many species of philodendron, grape ivy, begonias and many varieties of English ivy. Propagating in water alone is a very simple process, but be sure to change the water at regular intervals in order to maintain a good supply of free oxygen.

Other plants will root in sand or vermiculite, a more difficult process since it is necessary to keep the air about the cuttings moist. The double pot method (Fig. 23) is the simplest way to accomplish this. Take a 7″ or 8″ clay pot and, in the bottom, place a couple of inches of coarse gravel. Then fit a 3″, tightly-stopped clay pot in the center

Fig. 23: Double-pot arrangement for stem cuttings.

and pack the rooting medium between the two pots. (Caution: If vermiculite is used it must be compact, lest its drainage and aeration be diminished.) The cuttings are put in the rooting medium in concentric rings and water is flooded in to hold them in place. The smaller pot in the center serves as a well from which moisture will move by capillary attraction throughout the rooting medium. As the medium begins to dry out, the center pot can be refilled. To assure high humidity around the leaves, cover them with a dome of polyethylene plastic stretched over ribs made from coat hangers.

Most cuttings should form heavy root systems within six weeks. When there are several roots an inch or more in length the rooted cutting may be carefully lifted with a knife or trowel and potted in the proper soil mixture. Careful watering and shading are needed to help the new plants become established.

Mallet Cuttings

Plants with widely spaced leaves such as rubber plants and many of the philodendrons can be propagated by mallet cuttings. Actually, a mallet cutting is a stem section with a leaf attached, which receives its name from the fact that it resembles a mallet—the stem section as the head and the leaf as the handle. After making the cutting, wrap the stem section with moist sphagnum moss up to the base of the leaf petiole. Keep the moss damp at all times until roots shoot from the bud in the axil of the leaf. Then plant in the proper potting soil. A mallet cutting may also be rooted in the manner previously described for ordinary stem cuttings.

LEAF CUTTINGS

African violets, episcia, *Peperomia maculosa,* snake plants (*Sansevieria*) and watermelon begonias can be propagated by leaf cuttings. Select a healthy, firm but not quite full-grown leaf or, in the case of the snake plant, a portion of it. Cut the leaf off with a bit of the stem attached. Then firmly place the leaf cutting, stem part first, into a rooting medium of moistened sand. Use the double-pot arrangement to keep the sand moist (but not wet) until the cuttings are rooted and ready to be transplanted into the potting soil. The time required for a leaf cutting to form a heavy root system depends upon the kind of plant, the season and the environment into which the cutting is introduced.

DIVISION

Quite a few planter plants (including most ferns, snake plants, succulents, some ivies, cast-iron plant and leopard plants) multiply themselves in clumps and need only to be separated. In some cases the roots may simply be pulled apart giving each clump its own root system. With woody or massive plants, use a sharp knife to separate the clumps. Do as little cutting as possible and try to keep a generous amount of the root in proportion to the top growth. If the roots are small, cut back the top growth somewhat to maintain a good proportion. To pot the clumps, place them in the proper soil mixture and keep the pots out of direct sunlight and drafts until the roots are well established. Do not overwater the plant at the beginning, since the small root systems have a low absorption capacity, but don't go to the other extreme and let them dry out. To give the new plants the best possible humidity, place a large glass jar over the top of the pot. The plant can be gradually "hardened" to room air by removing the cover for increasingly long periods of time each day.

Many plants grow offsets, or suckers, which, if they have roots, may be pried loose and potted in the manner just described. Or they may be started like stem cuttings described earlier in this chapter.

LAYERING

There are two ways of propagating plants by layering—ground layering and air layering.

Ground Layering

This method of propagation is frequently used for the many species of ivies and philodendron that grow as vines.

Fill a 3″ or 4″ pot with either sand or vermiculite and place it next to the pot containing the mother plant. Then bend the stem or stems of the parent plant over to the new pot and staple them in a horizontal position on the rooting medium with hairpins. Keep the rooting medium moist and soon roots will form at each node. When the new plants are well rooted, sever them from the parent plant.

Air Layering

Air layering, Chinese layering or marcottage is a method used to increase *Ardisia crenulata,* dracaena, dieffenbachia, *Fatsia japonica,* fiddle-leaf plant, *Monstera deliciosa,* rubber plant, cordyline and screw pine. When these species have become "leggy" and shed their lower leaves, they can be given new root systems by this method. The new plant will have a more attractive habit of growth than it formerly displayed with its long stem. To accomplish air layering, a partial cut is made through the stem or a ring of bark is removed just below the leaf mass and a splinter inserted in this incision so that it does not grow shut. A mass of moist sphagnum moss the size of a baseball is placed around the stem where the incision was made. Kitchen-grade aluminum foil or polyethylene plastic film is used as a wrap to protect the layer, as shown in Fig. 24. (Complete air-layering kits with instructions are available at most florist shops and garden centers.) In the ball of moist sphagnum moss the roots will grow quickly and abundantly. When the ball is well filled with roots, sever the rooted portion from the parent plant. Then pot the new

Fig. 24: Method of wrapping to protect air layering.

plant in a soil mixture, adding more sand than is average for a first planting. Protect new plants as you would any plant: keep them out of direct sun and provide extra humidity until they are firmly rooted.

The best time to practice air layering is during the summer months when growth is at its best and the high temperatures and humidity contribute to quick rooting.

APPENDIX • Planter Equipment— A Buyers' Guide

The construction materials required to build planters can be purchased from your local hardware store or lumber yard. Local garden-supply houses, hardware dealers and mail-order suppliers are good sources for peat moss or sphagnum moss, pots, tubs, tools and plant foods.

Annual and perennial plants and seeds for exterior planters may be purchased locally or from national mail-order houses. Local florist shops, greenhouses and nurs-eries are the first place to look for the plants listed in Chapter 4. If you cannot find them there, you may wish to investigate (in person or by mail) one of the following sources:

GENERAL SUPPLIES

L. Sherman Adams Company, Benvenue Street, Wellesley 81, Massachusetts

Alberts & Merkel Bros., Inc., Route 6, Jackonsville 7, Florida

Armstrong Nurseries, Ontario, California

Arvida Orchids, P. O. Box 1467, South Miami, Florida

Barbara Lane Gardens, 22 North Voluntario Road, Santa Barbara, California

Barrington Greenhouses, P. O. Box 85, Barrington, New Jersey

Bill Hofmann Nursery, 2160 N.W. 79th Street, Miami, Florida

Breck's of Boston, 250 Breck Building, Boston 10, Massa-chusetts

Burgess Seed & Plant Company, Galesburg, Michigan

Castles of Florida, 1060 Terrace Boulevard, Orlando, Florida

Charmaine Gardens, 301 Allamandy, Lakeland, Florida

Dauerheim, Inc., Jerusalem & Wantagh Avenues, Wantagh, New York

Everglades Enterprises, Inc., P. O. Box 811-I.A.B., Miami, Florida

Fern Hawaiian Nursery, 1551 Avalon Boulevard, Wilmington, California

Fischer Greenhouses, Linwood, New Jersey

Fruitland Nursery, P. O. Box 910, Augusta, Georgia

Glen St. Mary Nursery, Glen St. Mary, Florida

George J. Bull, Inc., West Chicago, Illinois

George W. Park Company, Greenwood, South Carolina

Gries Floral Company, 11110 South Wallace Street, Chicago 28, Illinois

Havalook Gardens, 10045 West Grand River Avenue, Fowlerville, Michigan

Hawaiian Gardens, 1338 Kohou Street, Honolulu, Hawaii

House Plant Corner, Oxford, Maryland

James Rare Plant Nursery, 605 South San Jose Road, Campbell, California

John Beckner, Inc., 736 Myrtle Way South, St. Petersburg, Florida

Jayners, 5102 Seminole Avenue, Tampa 3, Florida

Julius Roehrs Company, 575 Paterson Avenue, East Rutherford, New Jersey

Kallman's Garden Nurseries, 418 Milpas, Santa Barbara, California

R. M. Kellogg Company, Three Rivers, Michigan

Lager & Hurrell, 424 Morris Avenue, Summit, New Jersey

Leon Ramirez Florists, 2519 San Bernardo Avenue, Laredo, Texas

Logee's Greenhouses, 55 North Street, Danielson, Connecticut

Lounsberry Gardens, Oakford, Illinois

Merry Gardens, 1 Simonton Road, Camden, Maine

E. W. McLellan Company, 1450 El Camino Road, San Francisco 25, California

Monroe Nursery, Monroe, Michigan

James W. Owen Nursery, Bloomington, Illinois

Pauer's Greenhouses, Route 1, Waukesha, Wisconsin

Pearce Seed Company, Moorestown, New Jersey

Plant Sales Nursery, 19 West Chicago Avenue, Hinsdale, Illinois

Reigle Gardens, 1675 South Floral Avenue, Bartow, Florida

River House, Inc., 20 Danbury Road, Wilton, Connecticut

Rivermont Orchids, Signal Mountain, Tennessee

Shaffer Nurseries, North Highland Avenue, Clearwater, Florida

Shoreline Nurseries, Inc., P. O. Box 453, Kennebunkport, Maine

Spoutz Greenhouses, 13310 State Fair, East, Detroit 51, Michigan

Stassen Floral Gardens, Department 17, Roslyn Heights, New York

Stern's Nurseries, Inc., Geneva, New York

Sunnybrook Gardens, South Lancaster Road, Reynoldsburg, Ohio

Terrace View Gardens, Greencastle, Indiana

Tinari's Floral Gardens, Valley Road & Route ⚹163, Bethayres, Pennsylvania

Tongg Ranch, P. O. Box 2113, Honolulu, Hawaii

C. H. Van Bourgondien, 1740 Fulton Avenue, East
Meadow, New York
Wayside Gardens, Mentor, Ohio
Wilson Brothers, Roachdale, Indiana
Wilson's Gardens, 943 Greenwood N.E., Atlanta, Georgia

READY-MADE PLANTER BOXES, TUBS, AND PLANT WALKERS

Denver Terra Cotta Company, 135 Tejon Street, Denver
23, Colorado
Gary Wood Products, 130 Neil Street, Memphis 12, Tennessee
Patio Wood Products, Inc., 835 Commercial Street, San
Gabriel, California
William Tricker, Inc., 3215 Brookside Avenue, Saddle
River, New Jersey

INDEX